Knowledge of Self: Understanding the Mind of the Black Male

Acknowledgments

Feared, vilified, hated, misunderstood, and admired, this book is dedicated to Black men who are seeking to shake off the chains and break the cycle of oppressed thought and behavior as well as the men and women who are helping our Black men and boys in this effort.

Introduction

You may be wondering, why write a book about what influences the psychology of the Black male? In modern-day society, we are inundated with messages that project Black men as dangerous, dumb, and deviant individuals. These messages are communicated via popular culture media that provide only a narrow view of the Black male experience. However, this view has created a "factual reality" that significantly influences how we think about Black men and how Black men think about themselves. The current text seeks to explore the components that comprise the Black male identity, including emotional development (alexithymia), ethnic identity, racial identity, the role of aggression, generational trauma, and gender norms.

I posit that the chronic internalization and perpetuation of negative stereotypes of Black males stem from the transmission of ways of thinking and behaviors that have been influenced by historical factors (e.g., slavery) and gender/racial-socialization processes. Specifically, these factors have influenced emotional development, the internalization of gender norms, and the use of aggression and anger in Black males. These factors are important in regards to executive functioning, decision making, and the maintenance of interpersonal relationships. In addition, constructs such as ethnic/racial identity can serve as buffers and potential modes of intervention.

The current text will also synthesize the empirical evidence in the scientific literature and the anecdotal experiences of Black males in an effort to develop a better understanding of the Black male psyche. Furthermore, this text will also explore the clinical implications of the convergence of these factors and how they may influence the presentation of mental illness in Black men. Lastly, in an effort to move past theory to application, this text provides a broad range of clinical interventions and activities that anyone who works with Black men across a variety of settings can use to address issues related to generational trauma, anger and aggression, emotional development, and racial identity development.

TABLE OF CONTENTS

ACKNOWLEDGEMENTS……………………………………...2
INTRODUCTION…..………………………………………....3

CHAPTER
  I. GENERATIONAL TRAUMA: TOO CALLOUSED TO CARE……………………………………………….6
  II. BLACK MANHOOD: OVERCOMING THE 3 D's (Dumb, Deviant, Dangerous) …………………………16
  III. ALEXITHYMIA: HOW YA FEELIN, BRUH?…...…………………………………………32
  IV. THE ROLE OF AGGRESSION: I RATHER DIE ON MY FEET THAN LIVE ON MY KNEES………......................42
  V. RACIAL/ETHNIC IDENITY: I AM WHATEVER I SAY I AM…….…………………………………..............54
  VI. BLACK MALE IDENTITY DEVELOPMENT SUMMARY……………………………………...…..97
  VII. BLACK MALE IDENTITY AND CLINICAL IMPLICATIONS FOR MENTAL HEALTH PROFESSIONALS…………...100
    DEPRESSION: SLIENT FUSTRATION………………………….........................103
    CLINCAL INTERVENTIONS………………………...106
    BIOGRAPHY……………………………………...…..124
  APPENDIX……………………………….……......126

Chapter 1

GENERATIONAL TRAUMA: TOO CALLOUSED TO CARE

The institution of slavery has chronically affected the experience of Black people in the United States. Slavery made explicit a way of thinking and behaving that endorsed the subjugation of a race of people based on characteristics such as skin color, facial features, religion, and ethnic background. To this day, Black people carry with them the legacy of slavery (e.g., food, ceremonies such as jumping the broom, and intragroup skin color discrimination). This legacy has significantly impacted how Black people (especially Black men) think about themselves as well as how popular culture perceives them within the societal framework. Although the legacy of slavery highlights the resiliency of the people of the African Diaspora, there exists the presence of maladaptive trauma-based ways of thinking and behaving that have been infused in the "psychological DNA" of Black individuals and passed down through the generations. This chapter will explore the influence of the intergenerational transmission of trauma (via slavery and chronic racism and discrimination) and its effect on the psychological experience of Black men.

Generational Trauma Overview

During the eighteenth century, the United States transformed itself into a "slave society" where slavery served as the economic engine for the vehicle of agricultural production and the White master–Black slave relationship provided a social framework that would have a ripple effect to this day. Within the context of slavery, Black people experienced unbearable grief related to the loss of cultural norms (e.g., language, religion, family, sense of self), the despair of loss of freedom, and the hopelessness and rage of physical violation and abuse. As Black people endured this experience, chronic emotions of shame, rage, and helplessness developed. From generation to generation, this constellation of emotional states has been passed down with each generation experiencing its own form of traumatization: from slavery to Jim Crow to "separate but unequal" and now the presence of covert racism and discrimination in present-day society.

This experience of re-traumatization is formally called secondary traumatization. Secondary traumatization refers to the effects of trauma on individuals who were traumatized indirectly by a traumatic event that a family member a generation prior had experienced. Secondary traumatization can significantly impact the children of previous trauma survivors. These individuals are more likely to experience distress in interpersonal relationships and more anger in their families of origin that manifests as emotional neglect and less secure attachment. Within the context of the intergenerational transmission of trauma between parent and child, less secure attachment can lead to a disorganized style of attachment between the dyad. Here, the parents are preoccupied with the pain they have experienced from their traumatic experiences (either ones they have seen from their parents or experienced themselves) and transmit this unresolved pain to their children. This disorganized attachment presents in one of two ways: "hostile/self-referential attachment" or "helpless–fearful attachment." A hostile/self-referential attachment style refers to parents who have experienced a traumatic event exhibiting contradicting rejecting behaviors together with behaviors that seek to receive attention from their children. An example of this attachment style would be a father who lost his mother as a child simultaneously criticizing his daughter and putting her down (rejection behaviors) while buying her things and seeking validation that he was a good father. A helpless–fearful attachment style refers to a parent who exhibits fearful, withdrawn, and inhibited behaviors (e.g., a woman's husband suddenly passes away and she becomes withdrawn from her son). In addition, individuals exposed to the intergenerational transmission of trauma develop a vulnerability to having poorer coping skills for future potentially traumatic events. Within this framework, unresolved parental traumatic experiences and losses lead to disruptive parental behavior (hostile/self-referential or helpless–fearful attachment), which contributes to distress and insecure attachment in the child (leaving them vulnerable to being overwhelmed by future traumatic events). With this understanding of the effect of the intergenerational transmission of trauma, the following paragraph will explore two areas important to understanding how trauma-related behaviors (e.g., family communication style and the emergence of post-traumatic stress symptomatology) and how these concepts relate to the psychological experience of Black men.

Two modes of communication have been identified in regards to the discussion of traumatic experiences: open verbal communication and knowing–not-knowing communication. Open verbal communication refers to having open discussion about traumatic experiences within the family. In regards to cultural trauma and Black men, this mode of communication would include discussions about the institution of slavery, racism and discrimination, the reoccurring experience of trauma, and how to manage trauma-related behaviors and ways of thinking. Knowing–not-knowing communication refers to the nonverbal presence of trauma-related experiences in the family that are maintained by a lack of open communication. For example, the father of a ten-year-old Black boy is killed by White police officers in what is believed to be a racially motivated shooting. The content of the shooting is communicated to the son, but the context is not (e.g., potential presence of racism and discrimination). Despite this absence of communication, the boy is still being communicated messages related to the trauma in regards to displaying emotions such as fear or sadness (e.g., not being allowed to cry at his father's funeral and being simultaneously rewarded and punished when engaged in conflicts with White authority figures) and the use of aggression to manage frustration related to perceived racism and discrimination. Furthermore, living with his grandmother (who does not discuss her son's death), the grandson keeps silent on the issue so as not to burden her with his grief about missing his father.

In an effort to protect their caregivers in the previous generation, many children will assume a posture of silence when indirectly exposed to the trauma experiences of prior generations. From the five-great grandmother witnessing her father whipped as a slave, to the grandfather who watched his father be beaten for sitting at a Whites Only table, to the present day where all a young Black boy has to do is turn on the TV to see that he has been labeled as a hypersexual, aggressive animal with limited intelligence, Black individuals have been exposed to trauma that they have learned to cope with in silence. However, this silence may be the primary vehicle through which the transmission of trauma-related behaviors and ways of thinking occurs across generations. The avoidance of dealing with the grief, shame, and guilt related to cultural trauma contributes to family dysfunction via the passing down of unspoken rules. These unspoken rules are related to the transmission of unclear messages including the institution of slavery, subsequent culturally traumatic experiences, their influence on the experience of racial and ethnic identity development, the perpetuation of the traditional masculine ideology, and trauma-related symptoms such as emotional numbness (alexithymia) and hypervigilance (anger and aggression). The following paragraph will explore further the effect of trauma-related symptoms on the intergenerational transmission of trauma-related behaviors and ways of thinking in Black men.

Generational Trauma and Black Males

The term "post-traumatic stress" quantifies a constellation of symptoms that an individual experiences when a traumatic event overwhelms their coping mechanisms. This paragraph will explore how these symptoms are associated with the intergenerational transmission of trauma-related behaviors and ways of thinking as well as highlight how these pseudo post-traumatic stress symptoms manifest within a family system. At the core of trauma-related symptoms is a chronic reliving of the trauma. From a cultural trauma perspective, Black males are constantly exposed to chronic acts of racism that reinforce their negative perceptions of themselves and other Black males. This exposure consists of overt acts (e.g., police brutality) that highlight second-class citizenship or covert acts (e.g., being told to focus on sports instead of school) that trap Black men in stereotypical boxes and regulate their potential to what society deems is appropriate for them.

Another symptom associated with cultural trauma is hypervigilance. Hypervigilance describes an intense mistrust of one's environment, causing them to always be on high alert for unsafe circumstances. For Black men, this has led to a certain level of paranoia of institutions and authority figures. From slave masters with the power to violate their wives and sell off their children to government-sanctioned events such as the Tuskegee Experiment, a message of mistrust and hypervigilance has been passed down from generation to generation of Black males. At the core of this hypervigilance are underlying feelings of shame, guilt, and rage: shame and guilt for not being able to protect their loved ones or themselves and rage towards authority figures for making them feel this way. This rage is the most transparent emotion associated with hypervigilance in Black males and is associated with acts of aggression or anger. However, due to conflicting messages concerning their power to use this anger and aggression for positive change (e.g., I am told not to trust the government because of what they did to Black people, but the government supports our family as well as removes my brothers and sisters if they feel my mom can't take care of us), Black men turn this anger and aggression on members of their own race (e.g., Black-on-Black violence) or on themselves via suicide and other self-harm behaviors (e.g., substance abuse).

An additional symptom associated with cultural trauma and trauma-related behavior is emotional numbing. Emotional numbing describes the experience of shutting out certain emotional states (e.g., sadness, fear) in an effort to lessen their distressing impact. The behavior of emotional numbing is transmitted through generations in relation to their experience of cultural trauma via messages such as "men don't cry" to toughen Black men up in the expectation of difficult lives ahead due to racism and discrimination. The intergenerational transmission of trauma has significantly impacted the experience of the Black male. Developed as a way to protect Black men from the effects of slavery and chronic racism and discrimination, these trauma-related behaviors and ways of thinking have communicated messages of hopelessness and despair that have manifested in the form of shame, guilt, rage, poor attachment, silence, and the development of confusing unspoken rules in families. At the individual level, trauma-related behaviors and ways of thinking appear as pseudo post-traumatic stress symptoms such as chronic reliving of the trauma, hypervigilance, and emotional numbing. This concept can be summarized via the following: institution of slavery → perpetuation of racial discrimination → increased vulnerability to post-traumatic stress symptoms → additional traumatic exposure → individual coping resources are overwhelmed and develops pseudo post-traumatic stress symptoms → transmission of trauma-related behaviors and ways of thinking. This process will be highlighted in the following example.

For example, there is a family unit that consists of a single mother and a ten-year-old son and his five-year-old brother. The son's biological father was killed three years prior due to gang violence. After his father's death, the son was told he was "the man of the house" and had to assume pseudo-parental responsibilities such as taking care of his little brother. Applying the concepts discussed earlier in the chapter, the son has been placed in a position where he has to share in a great deal of his mother's burdens (e.g., worrying about money, housing, keeping the family safe). In addition, highlighting the extension of intergenerational trauma, the mother's father was imprisoned for most of her life, influencing the messages she received about the role of Black men and the ones she passes down to her son.

Within this young man's framework are two competing ideologies about what it means to be a Black male (the invisible Black male vs. the idealized Black male) as well as sharing in his mother's trauma related to multiple losses. For the young man, the invisible Black male perspective implies that Black men hold a powerful role in their families via their absence (e.g., "If your father was here, we wouldn't be struggling as much"; "If your father was here, he would straighten you out and teach you how to be a man"). The idealized Black male highlights the wished-for Black male and the transmission of high expectations associated with the role of a Black male. However, the burden falls upon the child to fulfill this idealized role, which he perceives that his grandfather and father couldn't achieve.

By having to share this burden with his mother, the son is at an increased risk for developing trauma-related ways of behaving and thinking. If he seeks to fulfill the role of the idealized Black male, he will negate his own wants and needs in an effort to be the Black male for his mother that she did not receive from his grandfather or from his biological father. However, because he is only ten years old, he does not have the capacity to assume this role; this leads to feelings of shame (because he cannot live up to unrealistic expectations) and rage towards himself, his mother, and his father and grandfather. Because he cannot be upset with his mother (due to not wanting to burden her based on her experience of trauma), he turns his anger inward via experiences of self-hate as well as towards individuals who remind him of the legacy he cannot fulfill (e.g., other Black males). Consistent with the discussion in the current chapter, this way of thinking and behaving is maintained via the knowing–not-knowing silence in the family concerning the experience of multiple losses across generations as well as the disorganized attachment between mother and son (a carryover of the mother's cultural trauma from her father's imprisonment). Furthermore, pseudo post-traumatic symptoms emerge due to chronic concerns about safety and abandonment (hypervigilance), the development of a non-emotional posture to protect against feelings of fear and shame (emotional numbing), and a constant reliving of the trauma (e.g., the son reminding the mother of his biological father).

Intergenerational trauma has had a significant impact on the experience of Black men in the United States. Based on the messages passed down from the institution of slavery onward, Black men have internalized trauma-related ways of thinking and behaving that promote the hyper endorsement of a traditional masculine ideology, unresolved feelings of shame and guilt that manifest as expressions of self-hate towards themselves and other Black men, and pseudo post-traumatic behaviors such as hypervigilance and emotional numbing. The key to addressing this issue is to start an open dialogue within the family system about past generational traumas (e.g., talking about the impact of slavery, Jim Crow, chronic racism and discrimination) to help Black males make sense of the indirect messages they receive related to the cultural trauma (e.g., negative stereotypes, implicit messages about Black masculinity). By having this discussion, Black males will be able to differentiate themselves from negative cultural expectations and develop a coherent sense of self that integrates intergenerational messages as well as their own personal experiences.

Questions for Reflection

Think back to important events in your family's history. How have these events influenced how you think about the world?

What messages have been passed down through your family concerning the role of Black men?

How have these messages influenced how you think about yourself and other Black men?

How did you get your name? What messages do you think were being communicated by how you were named or whom you were named after?

Reference

Baranowsky, A. B. et al. (2013). PTSD transmission: A review of secondary traumatization in Holocaust survivor families. *Canadian Psychology, 39*(4) 247–256.

Frankish, T., & Bradbury, J. (2012). Telling stories for the next generation: Trauma and nostalgia. *Journal of Peace Psychology, 18*(3) 294–306.

Giladi, L., & Bell, T. (2013). Protective factors for intergenerational transmission of trauma among second and third generation Holocaust survivors. *Psychological Trauma: Theory, Research, Practice, and Policy, 5*(4), 384–391.

Gump, J. P. (2010). Reality matters: The shadow of trauma on African American subjectivity. *Psychoanalytic Psychology*, 27, 1, 4254.

Letzter-Pouw, S. E., Shira, A., Ben-Ezra, M., & Palgi, Y. (2013). Trauma transmission through perceived parental burden among Holocaust survivors' offspring and grandchildren. *Psychological Trauma: Theory, Research, Practice, and Policy*, doi:10.1037/a0033741.

Chapter 2

BLACK MANHOOD: OVERCOMING THE 3 D's (Dumb, Deviant, and Dangerous)

What does it mean to be a Black man? Being Black and male highlights the intersection between two layers of identity: race and gender. Furthermore, being a Black male also highlights the simultaneous process of the Black male experience being defined and negated within the societal context. From a cultural standpoint, Black males have a standing expectation of being the priest, provider, and protector in their homes. Additionally, at the more global level of masculinity, Black men are expected to endorse certain traditional masculine characteristics such as being non-emotional and aggressive. However, these expectations are negated by the chronic negative stereotypes and acts of racism and discrimination that Black males experience. This chapter will explore the definitions associated with traditional masculinity as a well as models that have been developed to explain the construct of Black masculinity. In addition, this chapter will explore how Black masculinity is learned within the context of the family system, peer groups, and prison culture. Lastly, this chapter will explore the impact of Black masculinity on the experience of anger and aggression, racial self-hate, and emotional restriction.

Masculinity Ideology and Black Manhood

Masculinity ideology has been defined as socially constructed standards of male behavior. This ideology develops as boys internalize certain cultural norms and expectations about socially acceptable male behavior within the context of the family system, peer groups, and the surrounding environment. One of the initial definitions of masculine ideology highlights four central standards: no sissy stuff, the big wheel, the sturdy oak, and give 'em hell. The no sissy stuff standard reflects the concern of avoiding femininity and emotional restriction. The big wheel standard notes the expectation of being the provider in the family and receiving the admiration and respect of peers and the community. The sturdy oak standard raises the concern of demonstrating toughness and a perpetual air of confidence across settings. Lastly, the give' em hell standard is the propensity towards violence, aggressiveness, and risk taking expected of males. Throughout the years of masculinity ideology research, social scientists have expanded upon these early definitions to include the presence of multiple masculine ideologies. Most relevant to the current discussion is the endorsement of a traditional masculine ideology.

Traditional masculinity is a strict adherence to the cultural norms and expectations for men such as competitiveness, physical and sexual violence, restricted emotionality, and the avoidance of all behavior deemed feminine by peer groups and popular culture. Interestingly, studies have demonstrated that Black men adhere the most to traditional masculine ideology in comparison to other races. However, based on this perceived masculinity, significant efforts have been made across history to undermine this sense of Black manhood. From castration during slavery and the Jim Crow era to covert institutional racism and discrimination, Black manhood has been viewed as a threat. This creates a cyclical pattern that includes (a) Black men being seen as hypermasculine; (b) efforts made to contain this Black manhood; (c) Black men experiencing the conflict of fulfilling traditional masculine roles and the impact of racism and discrimination on their ability to assume these roles; and (d) Black men engaging in hypermasculine behaviors, which supports the perceived endorsement of traditional masculinity in Black men and recreates the cycle. The following section will explore the models that have attempted to make sense of the inherent conflict in the development of Black masculinity (e.g., seeking to fulfill masculine roles and the perceived inability to assume these roles based on institutional and societal factors) and the creation of an alternative sense of manhood in anticipation of or in response to the experience of chronic racism and discrimination.

Development of Black Masculinity

As discussed in the previous section, masculinity represents the internalization of gender norms and standards that have been influenced by societal expectations and reinforced within the context of the family system, peer groups, and overarching environment. Some of these expectations include being a provider and protector, demanding and receiving respect, and projecting an air of confidence. For many Black males, there are significant barriers to fulfilling these roles. Black men are disproportionally represented in the criminal justice system (14% of the population, 42% of the prison population), undereducated (less than 8% of Black males have graduated from college), significantly at risk for death by homicide (Black males 18–24 comprise 51% of Black murder victims), and at an increased risk for leading lives filled with unemployment and poverty. The conflict between the expectation to adhere to traditional masculine roles and the overwhelming barriers that Black men face assuming these roles leaves Black men being in a constant state of having their masculinity questioned or defined in negative terms. This conflict leads to chronic reorganizing of gender identity in an effort to develop and maintain an alternative masculinity within this context. This section will explore a number of models that have been developed to describe this process.

Several studies have explored the development of gender identity and males. O'Neil and Carroll (1998) quantified a general model of gender identity development called Gender Role Journey theory. The Gender Role Journey theory consists of five phases: (1) acceptance of traditional gender roles, (2) ambivalence about gender roles, (3) anger over gender roles, (4) personal–professional activism, and 5.) celebration and integration of gender roles. In the first phase, acceptance of traditional gender roles, men rigidly adhere to gender stereotypes (e.g., aggression, emotional restriction). In phases 2 and 3, men experience cognitive dissonance due to their growing awareness that their rigid adherence to gender stereotypes have negatively contributed to social norms and expectations. These individuals experience confusion, anger, fear, and anxiety as they question their role ideology. Furthermore, in the fourth and fifth phases, men channel their anger into positive social activism. Many Black men get stuck in the middle phases because of the cycle of having to question their gender identity within the confines of a racially hostile environment that simultaneously perpetuates and rewards hypermasculinity in Black men while also seeking to punish or contain masculinity in Black men.

In regards to the development of Black masculinity specifically, a study by Hunter and Davis (1992) found that the development of Black masculinity occurs in a relational context. The researchers identified four domains associated with Black masculinity: self-determinism and accountability, family, pride, and spirituality and humanism. According to the researchers, self-determinism and accountability reflects five key components: (1) having a clear vision and ambition (directedness), (2) possessing the ability to make amends for past wrongs (maturity), (3) having economic stability (economic viability), (4) having mental toughness and resiliency (perseverance), and (5) having the ability to determine one's fate (free will). The family domain demonstrates the valuing of family responsibility and connectedness, egalitarian roles in male–female relationships, and the fulfillment of family role expectations. The pride domain involves having confidence in one's definition of Black masculinity and highlights the importance of self-improvement as an aspect of Black manhood. Lastly, the spirituality and humanism domain includes the interconnectedness that Black men have with the human community as well as the role of spiritual relatedness.

A study by Hammond and Mattis (2005), built on Hunter and Davis's (1992) theory of Black masculinity development by expanding the relational context and interconnectedness of the Black male manhood experience. The authors described four distinct ways in which Black masculinity is defined: an interconnected state of being, a fluid developmental process, a redemptive process, and proactivity. Having an interconnected state of being describes the process of constructing the meaning of Black manhood through spirituality, self-awareness, community, and family. Additionally, the development of Black manhood is a fluid process of continuous evaluation within this relational context. Furthermore, the development of Black manhood promotes a sense of responsibility towards active participation in one's family and community. Lastly, Black manhood is developed proactively as a protective factor against the barriers and challenges Black men face due to racism and discrimination and chronic exposure to negative stereotypes (Hammond & Mattis, 2005).

The last model of Black masculinity discussed in this section is the "cool pose." Coined by Majors and Billson (1992), the cool pose represents a constellation of behaviors exhibited by Black men as a demonstration of masculinity. Cool pose behaviors are reflected in physical posture, speech, style of clothing, mannerisms, restricted emotionality, and denial of vulnerability. According to the authors, these behaviors create an alternative form of masculinity to protect Black males from the deleterious effects of racism and discrimination. Majors and Billson also noted that while a cool pose posture reflects an attempt to overcome the negative stereotypes associated with being a Black male, significant endorsement can lead to a reliance on hypermasculine roles and values (1992). The conflicting reception that Black males receive while engaging in a cool pose posture often reinforces these behaviors. For example, a young Black male led to believe that he is powerless to change his circumstances (e.g., poverty, discrimination) will be reinforced to assume a cool pose when his demeanor, style of clothing, and aggressiveness cause people to fear him (giving him some control or power in a perceivably powerless situation).

The development of Black manhood is a conscious raising process through which Black males seek to integrate sociohistorical and economically influenced expectations of masculinity. The previous models suggest that this process is significantly affected by contextual factors such as family of origin, peer groups, prison culture, and the media (Powell-Hammond & Mattis, 2005; Hunter & Davis, 1992; Majors & Billson, 1992). Within this context, the development of a hypermasculine identity stems from a reactionary attempt to create an alternative masculine identity in the face of chronic efforts to denigrate Black manhood. The following section will explore further the specific contextual factors that influence the development of Black manhood (e.g., family, peer group) with an initial discussion of the general reference groups Black men may use.

Reference Groups and Black Masculinity

Noting the importance of developing Black manhood within a relational context, several resources have sought to quantify the impact of reference groups (groups that Black men look to evaluate and adjust their perception of masculinity and masculine behaviors). Wade (1998) utilized the term male reference group identity dependence to describe individuals who rely heavily on reference groups to develop their conceptualization of Black masculinity. Wade (1998) highlighted three reference group identity-dependent statuses within this framework: no–reference group status, the reference group–dependent status, and the reference group–non dependent status. The no–reference group status is characterized by having a lack of psychological relatedness to other men. These individuals develop undefined or fragmented concepts of Black masculinity because they have no framework to draw from. The reference group–dependent status reflects individuals who exhibit relatedness to men in their in-group and no relatedness to individuals perceived to be in the out-group. These men will rigidly adhere to in-group expectations to the point of engaging in conformist, stereotyped, and rigid behaviors (Wade, 1998). An example would be the Black male whose in-group adheres to the mantra "live by the gun, die by the gun," suggesting the fact that the slightest provocation (e.g., a dirty look, a shove, a scuffed shoe) must be addressed swiftly and with a high level of violence "to teach a lesson and gain respect." The Black male with a reference group–dependent status would be obligated to react violently at the slightest perception of disrespect to maintain his in-group status because of his dependence on their reference norms for his self-concept. Lastly, the reference group–nondependent status characterizes men who have established a sense of commonality and connectedness with all men. These individuals' sense of Black masculinity is not dependent on a male reference group and adherence to rigid stereotyped norms. Instead, Black masculinity is internally defined with the inclusion of multiple fluid identities.

Franklin (1987) also examined the influence of reference groups on the development of Black masculinity. The researcher noted three types of reference groups that influence male role behavior within the context of Black masculinity: the Black man's peer group, sub-cultural reference group, and societal reference group. The peer group is characterized by the hypermasculine adaptation Black men make due to the experience of racism and discrimination. Franklin (1987) noted that norms within this reference group include antifemininity; aggressive solutions to disputes; contempt for beliefs, values, and rules that are oppressive towards Black men; and antagonism towards other Black men. The sub-cultural reference group includes the Black community as a whole and reflects the conflict in assuming a hypermasculine identity (to fit in with peer groups and defend against racism and discrimination) and demonstrating more nontraditional gender roles that promote solidarity within the Black community. The last reference group, societal reference group, describes the overarching social context in which norms and expectations of masculinity are internalized and reinforced or rejected.

Both Wade (1998) and Franklin (1987) highlight the influence of reference groups in regards to the development of Black masculinity in the internalization of traditional masculine norms. In an effort to carve out a sense of identity in a society inundated with negative images and perceptions of Black men, these individuals seek to identify with in-groups that adhere to rigid norms and promote and encourage hypermasculine behaviors. These behaviors are simultaneously vilified (Black male harming a White individual), reinforced (Black male celebrated for a vicious hit in a football or boxing match), and ignored (Black male murders another Black male). With no internally defined sense of masculinity, these individuals are at the mercy of their respective in-groups to find a place of acceptance and respect. The following section will explore three significant contextual groups that influence the Black male's adherence to rigid traditional masculine norms (family, peers, prison culture).

The family system is the initial context in which the seeds of defining Black masculinity are planted. Through the communication of implicit and explicit messages, Black men receive their initial lessons concerning how to manage anger and conflict, their role in interpersonal and romantic relationships, fatherhood and responsibility, as well as the challenges of being a Black male. As noted prior, within the family system, the role expectations communicated to Black men include being the provider, protector, and priest. However, due to significant challenges influenced by the experience of racism and discrimination (e.g., high unemployment rate, underrepresentation in academic achievement, overrepresentation in the justice system), how Black men learn to fulfill these roles highlights the creation of an alternative form of masculinity. For example, a Black father is attempting to help his young son learn the importance of being a good provider for his family. However, because the father has a felony on his record, his employment opportunities are severely limited. The father turns to alternative forms of making money (e.g., selling drugs) and ultimately ends up going back to prison (leaving his family to continue to struggle financially). Within this context, the young man learns that a Black male must provide for his family by any means. However, the outcome of the father's experience teaches him that this effort is ultimately futile because some Black men are caught in a lose–lose situation where they are denied the ability to seek out adaptive ways to fulfill their expected roles learned in the family.

Within the family context, there is a significant relational component to the development of Black masculinity. Black men learn and maintain their views of masculinity within the context of those individuals they have built relationships with. For example, reexamining the prior scenario, the young man's Black masculinity may be influenced by an uncle who is able to step in in his father's absence and provide an example that counters the lose–lose perception that he has developed based on his father's experience. This uncle, who has been exposed to the same forms of racism and discrimination, found a way to navigate these challenges in a way that is adaptive and fulfills the roles expected of him. Through this relationship, the uncle teaches the young man the importance of his relationship with himself (priest/spirituality), with his family (provider by stepping in in the father's absence), and with his environment (protector through teaching him how to navigate the experience of being a Black male in a possibly hostile world). These examples highlight the significance of the family in regards to developing Black masculinity. Additionally there is an important interdependence inherent in this process via defining masculinity not only through self but through family and as discussed in the following section through peers.

Peers are an integral part of the development of masculinity in Black males. If the family system is the initial classroom through which Black males learn the core tenets of masculinity, then peer groups are the field experience through which they test and refine their definition of Black masculinity. The importance of peer groups is highlighted in regards to their influence on the requirements for respect, acceptance, and in group identification among Black males. When faced with unattainable respect or denial from out-group members, the respect from in-group members or peers becomes even more important. However, the requirements for this respect can pose significant challenges. These requirements can include protecting the in-group from out-group intrusion or influences, following group norms, and knowing one's role within the group with appropriate aspirations of ascending the hierarchy (based on adherence to values deemed important to group members). Black males' inherent distrust of institutions coupled with the negative messages they receive from popular culture provide a fertile ground for the development of a doctrine of Black masculinity that is impenetrable to challenge and different perspectives. This "cultural fortress" insulates Black males from internalizing alternative messages of Blackness via the attainment of knowledge they can use to challenge peer norms (e.g., other avenues to success besides athletics, education isn't a White thing, assertiveness is a viable substitute for aggression). The prevention of an alternative perspective creates a cycle of reinforcement in which Black males engage in peer-normed behavior (e.g., get in multiple fights at school) and are simultaneously rejected by the institution (e.g., Black male joins the ranks of the many suspended from school or regulated to special education classes) and rewarded by their peer group for "not wasting time with that White folk stuff and handling business like a man."

    Infused within the prison-culture mindset are messages that are internalized by Black men concerning the utility of aggression and violence, the need for emotional restriction, limited interpersonal relationships, the chronic need to prove one's manhood through material gain and sexual conquest, the perpetuation of a pseudo self-determinism, and the unwritten "man code." The irony of this phenomenon lies in the fact that many of the messages that contribute to the internalization of a prison-culture mindset are also required to survive in the prison context. Thus, the rehabilitative assumption of the criminal justice system reinforces the very behaviors it was designed to suppress. In addition, within the greater society, these messages are given a very visible platform via the media and popular culture. The following paragraph will explore the construction of masculinity within the prison-culture context and discuss its ramifications for the overall development of Black masculinity.

    Due to the expected societal norms for masculinity, Black men are constantly pressed toward a heightened in-group conformity which is fueled by a perpetual overcompensation for a denigrated sense of manhood. Within the prison-culture mindset, an in-group conformity is reflected in actions related to reputation management, violence and aggression, and adherence to the man code. Within the prison-culture mindset, reputation management is the most important tool for survival, and all behaviors are geared towards the maintenance of one's "rep." At the core of this rep is a demonstrated sense of mastery over one's self and one's environment. For many Black men, the typical route for demonstrating mastery (e.g., educational attainment, career advancement) has been denied, leading to the search for alternate methods of exhibiting mastery. For example, a young Black male who has been expelled from school due to disruptive behavior is faced with limited options due to a lack of education. These limitations contribute to challenges in supporting his family origin. Because he is unable to financially support his family (stereotype associated with masculinity), he looks to other ways to demonstrate his mastery (e.g., being hypervigilant in protecting his block or turf from out-group members). Within this context, the young man's rep is based on this alternate sense of mastery (protecting his turf) and the method in which he demonstrates this form of mastery (hypervigilance and aggression). However, as noted prior, these behaviors reflect the experience of pseudo self-determinism because of the constant reminders of the superficial nature of the Black male's experience of mastery (e.g., institutional involvement in the form of the justice system and housing authority). Another aspect of the prison-culture mindset, and a significant component of reputation management, is the use of aggression and violence.

A more in-depth exploration of the influence of anger and aggression on Black masculinity will be the subject of the following chapter. However, within the context of understanding the role of violence and aggression in prison culture, this construct has a significant impact. Many Black men who engage in reputation-management behaviors and adhere to traditional masculine norms view the use of aggression as the only way to establish and maintain a viable rep. Within this context, fear and respect are synonymous, and there is a strong belief that you can't have one without the other. Within the prison-culture mindset, a viable rep is built on the amount of fear that one can induce in people via actual acts of aggression or the perceived possibilities of one's aggressive behavior. Popular culture reinforces the endorsement of this mindset via constant reminders of society's fear of Black men due to their inherent "aggressive nature." Similar to the construct of violence and aggression, another significant component that is reinforced within the prison culture mindset is the adherence to the man code. "I ain't no punk." "I keep it 100." "Ain't nobody taking mines." These sayings serve as descriptors for a way of being that reflects a strict adherence to traditional masculine norms (e.g., man code). One's adherence to the man code ideology is a perquisite to be a part of the in-group associated with the prison-culture mindset. However, one's membership in this in-group is up for review on an ongoing basis requiring constant testing of the individual's knowledge and willingness to engage in man code behaviors. This phenomenon puts the Black male in the position of always having to prove his manhood. For example, a young Black male may be constantly tested by his peers to demonstrate his adherence to the man code by engaging in fights to protect the in-group or witnessing illegal activity and being reminded of the consequences for snitching. In regards to the overarching discussion of the socialization (or learning process) of Black masculinity, the Black male learns that while the prison-culture mindset in-group may be the only in-group he feels able to relate to, there is a significant amount of variability in his membership status that requires the constant demonstration of acts of manhood with increasing intensity.

    Black masculinity is a fluid developmental construct with the specific task of providing Black men with the protective factors to address the chronic experience of racism and discrimination. Black men are constantly bombarded with conflicting messages concerning their experience of manhood. In the media and popular culture, Black men are often perceived as being dangerous, deviant, and dumb. This perception is reinforced by the limited images of the diversity of the Black male experience as well as the encouraged endorsement of a traditional masculine ideology. As noted prior, this process creates a cyclical pattern in which Black men are simultaneously denigrated and rewarded for adhering to these role expectations. In the face of this conflict and the perceived challenges in fulfilling the stereotypical male role, Black men have sought to develop an alternative masculinity that includes the endorsement of hypermasculine traits such as emotional restriction and the chronic use of aggression and violence.

    Black masculinity is relationally constructed with a significant emphasis on messages received from the family of origin as well as adherence to in-group norms. Within these settings Black men learn role expectations within a family system (e.g., priest, provider, and protector) as well as the rules for survival as a Black man and the requirements for in-group acceptance (e.g., protecting the in-group from out-group intrusion or influences, following group norms). These messages from the in-group are reinforced via the internalization of the prison-culture mindset. As noted previously in this chapter, the prison-culture mindset represents a heightened sense of group conformity via a perpetual overcompensation for a denigrated sense of manhood. All behaviors associated with this mindset are designed to facilitate the development of a viable rep and to prove one's adherence to a traditional masculine ideology.

To combat the challenges highlighted in regards to the development of Black masculinity, a number of issues must be addressed. First, the inherent conflict between community, peer, and media definitions of Black masculinity must be discussed. Secondly, the protective value of the endorsement of hypermasculine behaviors must be acknowledged within the context of building an alternative sense of manhood as well as searching for an in-group identification and acceptance. Third, the maladaptive nature of holding these beliefs must be made explicit. Lastly, Black men must be exposed to the concept of multiple masculinities in which they do not have to be regulated to a narrow definition of Black manhood. Instead, Black men can develop a core sense of manhood that is created within a relational context, but is ultimately defined by them allowing for more adaptive versions of hypermasculine behaviors (e.g., assertiveness vs. aggression).

Questions for Reflection

What does it mean to you to be a Black man?

What traits or qualities are associated with being a Black male?

How did you learn your definition of Black masculinity?

How do your peers and family define Black masculinity?

What are some examples of the prison-culture mindset that you have seen in your environment or in the media?

Reference

Hunter, A. G., & Davis, J. E. (1992). Constructing gender: An exploration of African American men's conceptualization of manhood. *Gender and Society, 6*, 464–479.

Franklin, I. I. C. W. (1987). Surviving the institutional decimation of Black males: Causes, consequences, and intervention. In H. Brod (Ed.), *The making of masculinities: The new men's studies.* Boston, MA: Allen and Unwin.

Majors, R., & Billson, J. M. (1993). *Cool pose: The dilemmas of Black manhood in America.* New York, NY: Simon & Schuster.

O'Neil, J. M., & Roberts Carroll, M. (1988). A gender role workshop focused on sexism, gender role conflict, and the gender role journey. *Journal of Counseling & Development, 67*, 193–197.

Powell-Hammond, W. & Mattis, J. S. (2005). Being a man about it: Manhood meaning among African American men. *Psychology of Men and Masculinity, 6*(2), 114–126.

Schwing, A.E., Wong, Y.J., & Fann, M.D. (2013). Development and validation of the African American men's gendered racism stress inventory. *Psychology of Men and Masculinity, 14*(1), 16–24.

Wade, J. C. (1998). Male reference group identity dependence: A theory of male identity. *The Counseling Psychologist, 26*, 349–383

Chapter 3

ALEXITHYMIA: HOW YA FEELIN, BRUH?

Alexithymia describes a chronic condition in which an individual has lost the ability to identify and describe emotions in oneself as well as the ability to understand emotional states in others (Levant et al., 2003). Due to experiences such as chronic generational trauma, the saturation of stereotypical behavior in the media, and invisible male role models, many of our Black men have become alexithymic. Having to suppress emotions as a protective factor or to support society's definition of how a "real" Black man acts, many Black men have resorted to acts of self-hate (e.g., Black-on-Black crime, abuse, and underachieving academically and professionally) as a way to cope with their unexpressed selves. This chapter will explore the development of alexithymia and how it impacts the psychology of Black males.

Alexithymia Overview

Based on the traditional masculinity ideology prevalent in the United States, men are bombarded with social messages that "less is more" in regards to emotional expression. From childhood on, men have been discouraged from expressing and talking about their emotions by members of their families of origin, popular culture and media, peers, and other men. Within Western society, this restricted emotional expression is believed to be used to establish and maintain a patriarchal power structure and hide evidence of vulnerability (Fischer & Good, 1997). The reinforcement of this socialization contributes to men experiencing an underdeveloped vocabulary for, and unawareness of, "unacceptable" emotions (e.g., shame, sadness, fear). The phenomenon of emotional restriction in men has been quantified in the psychological literature as alexithymia. The term alexithymia was introduced in the 1970s and describes challenges in the areas of emotional development including identifying and describing feelings, discerning the emotional states and displaying empathy in interpersonal relationships, and an externally focused style of thinking (Levant et al., 2009).

In regards to the etiology (potential factors that cause a disorder) for alexithymia, most theories have focused on biological (e.g., deficits in the emotion-processing structure in the brain) or social explanations (Parker et al., 2008). However, since the introduction of the concept of alexithymia over 40 years ago, the overarching understanding of alexithymia has moved towards highlighting the underlying social processes that contribute to emotional expression and understanding for men (Frewen et al., 2012). There is a general assumption in popular culture that when it comes to emotional restriction, men are "just born that way." However, there is evidence to suggest that boys start off with equal emotional regulation and expression to that of girls. Consistent with the socialization process, boys become less verbally expressive than girls around age 2 and less facially expressive by 6 years of age (Levant et al., 2009). This process is significantly influenced by the introduction of a traditional masculine ideology.

The traditional masculine ideology states that men must adopt dominant and aggressive behaviors and function within the public sphere. Within this framework, boys and men are constantly reminded of the need for emotional restriction as a requisite for manhood via messages such as "Big boys don't cry," "Man up," "Don't be a wuss," "Crying is for sissies," and "Tears are just weakness leaving the body." On some level, alexithymia has adaptive functions. For example, if one grows up in an unsafe environment and is chronically exposed to traumatic events, then regulating one's emotions to a select few can serve as a protective factor (e.g., anger and aggression now and sadness much later). However, this way of managing emotions can contribute to significant challenges in personal relationships and family of origin (e.g., estrangement from children and domestic violence), which will be explored in the following section.

High levels of alexithymia is considered a possible vulnerability factor for experiencing a variety of symptoms of psychological distress (Levant et al., 2003). Alexithymia has been found to be associated with the tendency to experience chronic anxiety, anger, and feelings of shame and embarrassment (Levant et al., 2009). These feelings are due in part to having a lower opinion of their abilities and a lack of motivation to follow through with set goals. The constellation of emotions occurs in a circular pattern that is influenced by the individual's challenges in emotional awareness. For example, a young man is in the middle of giving a presentation at school, and he sees two peers in the back of the class huddled together laughing. He interprets that their laughter is directed towards him because of his perceived poor speaking skills. As he makes this interpretation, he feels his heart start to race, and his face gets hot. These are often viewed as signs of feeling anxious, but to admit to being anxious would be to acknowledge a level of vulnerability that is not acceptable in the traditional masculine ideology. Instead, the physical symptoms of anxiety are interpreted as "My heart is racing; I must be angry," and he proceeds to yell at his peers and turn over a desk. Following this episode, the individual finds out that the peers were not laughing at him, and he begins to experience feelings of shame and embarrassment because of his reaction (that a combination of gender norms and alexithymia prevented him from recognizing).

Alexithymia has also been found to be associated with the perception of an external locus of control. External locus of control refers to the belief that factors outside of oneself (e.g., fate, luck) ultimately determine one's experience of success (or no success) in life. This mode of thinking is a hallmark of alexithymia and suggests a limited ability in regards to self-reflection and understanding internal states (e.g., emotions). These individuals come to believe that others control or significantly influence their emotions (e.g., "They were trying to make me angry") with an emphasis on those emotions that are socially acceptable and disregarding negative emotions that may be stirred up by these interactions. A belief in an external locus of control can lead to the development of a passive coping style (e.g., denial or blaming) and feelings of hostility.

Alexithymia has also been linked with impulsivity contributed to an automatic desire to rid oneself of tension resulting from disagreeable emotional states (Frewen et al., 2012). For example, revisiting the previous scenario concerning public speaking, whenever the individual hears about giving speeches or doing presentations, he starts to get a pain in his stomach (a possible sign of fear or anxiety). Without a developed emotional vocabulary, the individual interprets this pain as anger. With an external locus of control, the individual will feel that others may be controlling his stomach pain and anger by intentionally talking about a subject that creates significant tension for him. In response, he adopts a passive coping style that is impulsively manifested (e.g., blaming others for the response of anger without acknowledging the underlying shame and embarrassment about his perception of his speaking ability). This example highlights how alexithymia and underdeveloped emotional abilities can contribute to tension and discomfort via misinterpretation or lack of awareness of emotional states. This misinterpretation and lack of awareness is significantly influenced by the overarching masculine ideology that has been passed down via social leaning from generation to generation of men. Alexithymia can have adaptive functions in regards to the minimization of emotional discomfort and inoculation against negative emotions when faced with a traumatic experience as well as social acceptance due to an adherence to gender norms (Frewen et al., 2008). However, as noted in the previous example, alexithymia can contribute to the belief of an external locus of control and the development of a passive coping style that becomes generalized and automatically implemented across situations. The following section will explore the convergence of alexithymia and gender norms in Black males and how these constructs influence emotional development and its expression.

Black Males and Alexithymia

"Aloof," "cool," "hard to read," "indifferent," "apathetic," these have all been terms that are oftentimes used to describe interactions with Black men. Consistent with the current text's theme of the generational transmission of trauma as a way to quantify modes of thinking and behavior, Black men exhibit an increased risk for the experience of alexithymia (in part due to the historical aspects of slavery and the chronic experience of racism and discrimination). For over 400 years, Black people were taken from their countries of origin, transported like cattle across the ocean, inspected and sold, stripped of their native culture, and forced into a lifetime of servitude with the constant threat of abuse and death. In this context, being alexithymic, or displaying emotional restraint, was modeled as a way to survive. It was important to not become attached in personal relationships, because one never knew when the person might be sold or killed. Displaying sadness would have been too overwhelming considering the magnitude of trauma these individuals experienced on a daily basis. In addition, anger couldn't be shown for fear of harm coming to one's self or family. Instead, it was more beneficial to "keep them guessing" in regards to emotional expression.

    This mode of thinking has been passed down from generation to generation of Black men to help manage the chronic experience of racism and discrimination. However, several problems have arisen due to the experience of alexithymia in Black males. First, the art of keeping them guessing has been turned inward in the form of the underdevelopment of emotional awareness. Secondly, through the social learning process and the internalization of a traditional masculine ideology, many Black men have become disconnected from their own emotional selves. As noted previously, this disconnection can contribute to the perception of an external locus of control (feelings of hopelessness about one's situation), the development of a passive coping style for emotionally charged situations, impulsive behavior in a desire to rid oneself of disagreeable emotional states, and chronic feelings of anxiety and anger that manifest as hostility towards oneself and others.

    As an example, let's examine the influence of alexithymia over three generations of Black men that include a grandfather, a father, and a teenage son. The grandfather was a teenager during the 1930s and remembers listening to stories from his grandfather about slavery. In all of these stories, the grandfather was told of the importance of being strong for the family as the man and that this often meant doing things without letting one's emotions get involved. As the grandfather grows up, he experiences second-class citizenship with a singular story that highlights this experience involving his father. He remembers as a child going to a restaurant with his father and the waiter stating that they would have to go to the back of the store because they didn't serve his kind of people. Once in the back, their food was tossed on the ground and the father was forced to pick it up. The grandfather acknowledges how traumatic this event was but notes that what stuck out to him was seeing his father shed a tear for the first and only time in his life. He also mentions that his father told him that his lot as a Black man was set and that there was nothing he could do about it. Based on his childhood experiences and the influence of the men in his life, he has simultaneously learned that his role as a man is to be strong for his family but that he is powerless to fulfill this role. In addition, he has learned that emotions are painful, involve shame, and only get in the way of fulfilling one's role as a man. This emotional experience becomes a part of his "emotional DNA" and is passed down through the generations to his son and then to his grandson.

On some levels, as this example points out, being alexithymic had adaptive value for the family. It allowed them to keep going during very challenging times. However, as the context changed (e.g., dealing with racism and discrimination to raising a son or having a wife) the way of managing emotions did not. Similar to a fever simultaneously serving an important health function (e.g., immune system fighting an infection) as well as contributing to significant discomfort and possible extension of illness, alexithymia is a factor that has lost some of its protective value. As a fever turns on the body, alexithymia has contributed to the Black male's psyche turning inward via the tension experienced from ignoring negative emotions (shame, guilt, and fear) that are manifested as hostility and anger towards self and others. The teenage son in the aforementioned example may impulsively lash out at others because he carries the historical shame and guilt that his grandfather and his grandfather experienced. In addition, he may adopt a sense of hopelessness about his ability to change his circumstances. This creates an unbearable amount of conflict between the societal expectations as a man (e.g., independent and powerful) and the cultural messages that he has received in regards to his "place" as a Black man. To address this phenomenon, we must help Black men see the historical ramifications of the legacy of slavery and racism and discrimination and how it has specifically influenced the internalization of a traditional masculine ideology and emotional development. Furthermore, it will be important to help Black men find the words to describe their emotional experience.

Questions for Reflection

What were the rules for expressing emotion in your home?

Were there consequences for showing sadness or depression (e.g., crying)?

How do you feel that being a Black male influences your ability to show emotion?

How do you communicate your emotions to others? How do other people know you are angry? Sad?

What emotions are you most comfortable displaying?

What emotion are you least comfortable displaying?

How has anger and aggression affected your life?

Reference

Aust, S. et al. (2013). The role of early emotional neglect in alexithymia. *Psychological Trauma: Theory, Research, Practice, and Policy, 5*(3), 225–232.

Fischer, A. R. & Good, G. E. (1997). Men and psychotherapy: An investigation of alexithymia intimacy, and masculine gender roles. *Psychotherapy, 34*(2), 160–170.

Frewen, P. A. et al. (2008). Clinical and neural correlates of alexithymia in posttraumatic stress disorder. *Journal of Abnormal Psychology, 117*(1), 171–181.

Frewen, P. A. et al. (2012). Disturbances of emotional awareness and expression in posttraumatic stress disorder: Meta-mood, emotion regulation, mindfulness, and interference of emotional expressiveness. *Psychological Trauma: Theory, Research, Practice and Policy, 4*(2), 152–161.

Levant, R. F. et al. (2003). A multicultural investigation of masculinity ideology and alexithymia. *Psychology of Men and Masculinity, 4*(2) 91–99.

Levant, R. F. et al. (2009). Gender differences in alexithymia. *Psychology of Men & Masculinity, 10*(3), 190–203.

Parker, J. D. et al. (2008). Latent structure of the alexithymia construct: A taxometric investigation. *Psychological Association, 20*(4), 385–396.

Thomas, R. et al. (2011). Pathways from child sexual abuse to adult depression: The role of parental socialization of emotions and alexithymia. *Psychology of Violence, 1*(2), 123–135.

Zimmermann, G. et al. (2005). Alexithymia assessment and relations with dimensions of personality. *European Journal of Psychological Assessment, 21*(1), 23–33.

Chapter 4

THE ROLE OF AGGRESSION: I RATHER DIE ON MY FEET THAN LIVE ON MY KNEES

"Live by the gun, die by the gun," "Ain't nobody gonna take my manhood," "I rather die on my feet than live on my knees," "Fear is for the weak," each of these sayings highlights the socialization that Black men experience in regards to the expectation of control and diminishing the factor of fear via the use of anger and aggression. As noted in the chapter on Black masculinity, anger and aggression are considered instrumental to the development of a coherent masculine identity. For Black men, the use of anger and aggression has received conflicting responses in the context of family, peer groups, and popular culture. On the one hand, the use of aggression is celebrated in the greater society. When a Black male uses his aggression to help his team win a game or knock out an opponent in boxing, he is rewarded with praise and encouragement to continue this behavior. However, the Black male simultaneously receives a completely different message about the use of aggression outside of these arenas. In popular culture, the image of the "scary Black male" has been imprinted onto the very fabric of society.

Through the media as well as the endorsement of an aggressive posture by Black men themselves, a culture has been created with the expectation that Black men are dangerous individuals with an insatiable desire to engage in aggressive behaviors. This expectation has been internalized into the collective consciousness of society with most individuals instinctively responding to the phenomenon of Black male aggression with a fear response when in the presence of a Black male (e.g., clutching purse). A circular pattern is cocreated by this experience of Black male aggression in which a chronically denigrated segment of the population is exposed to feelings of power gained through the blunt instrument of aggression. This aggression produces a chronic state of fear that becomes integrated into the overarching perception of Black manhood. Seeking to maintain this position of influence, Black men create a standard of aggression that is adopted into the man code. As a Black male's identity develops, he is taught to rigidly adhere to this standard via praise and encouragement from his peer group, as well as the experience of fear he perceives in members of the out-group. However, with his masculinity constantly being challenged, the Black male is forced to display greater acts of fear inducing aggression. Thus, the Black male is regulated to a limited posture of hyper-aggression that perpetuates the stereotype of the "scary Black man." All the while, the Black male is compelled to engage in aggressive behaviors to achieve some semblance of power in society as well as the respect and acceptance of his peer group.

The current chapter will explore the concept of aggression and its influence on Black male identity development. Specifically, this chapter will facilitate a discussion focusing on three main areas: aggression as a generational trauma-coping response via hypervigilance, the use of aggression as an overcompensation response via social conditioning based on in-group norms, and the experience of displaced aggression due to chronic powerlessness and hopelessness. This chapter will conclude with a discussion concerning the use of assertiveness, as opposed to an overreliance on aggression, for conflict resolution.

Aggression has been defined as a behavior intended to harm another person (Reijntjes et al., 2013). At its most basic level, there are two main forms of aggression (verbal and non-verbal). Essentially, verbal aggression involves using words to hurt while non-verbal aggression consists of the more physical aspects of aggressive behavior. Sprankle, End, and Bretz (2012) highlighted three overarching avenues through which aggressive behavior is learned: cultivation, priming, and social learning.

Cultivation indicates that the more a person observes aggressive behavior in the media, the more likely he or she is to believe that the media-depicted images are consistent with reality. For example, a child who views a significant amount of violent images on TV or through video games may come to believe that violence is positively rewarded and that there are no long-term effects for aggressive behavior. In thinking about Black males, due to the oversaturation of violent and aggressive Black men in popular culture, these individuals' perceptions of Black men are altered to think that hyperaggressive masculinity should be the norm.

According to the authors, priming suggests that the more often an individual is exposed to images of aggressive behavior, the more salient aggression becomes. For Black males, this involves a hypervigilance for perceived acts of aggression as well as hyperaggression serving as the "go-to coping skill" when faced with distressing or overwhelming situations. Lastly, social learning is based on the premise of modeling and reinforcement. An individual is more likely to engage in a behavior when they see someone they respect receive a positive reward for this behavior. For a Black male, this may involve modeling the behavior of Black men they see on TV or in their neighborhoods. With the construct of respect having such a high value (but positive methods of achieving this respect deemed inaccessible), Black men will look to these individuals who have achieved respect through alternative means (e.g., hyperaggression, fear). The following section will explore three ways in which aggression influences the Black male experience: generational trauma and hypervigilance, peer group norms, and displaced aggressive behavior.

In chapter one, this text facilitated a discussion concerning the experience of intergenerational trauma and how this concept influences Black male identity development. Within this context, it was noted that many behaviors that Black men engage in (e.g., emotional restriction) are an extension of learned ways of coping with cultural traumas. These responses have been passed down through several generations of the Black male's family of origin and are consistently reinforced via the chronic experience of racism and discrimination. The trauma response most relevant to the current discussion in regards to aggression is hypervigilance.

Hypervigilance describes a heightened awareness of potentially dangerous situations. After experiencing a traumatic event, many individuals feel a high level of powerlessness because of their perceived inability to keep the traumatic experience from happening. These individuals develop a posture of chronic awareness to compensate for these feelings of vulnerability. Eventually, instead of providing compensation, this chronic awareness causes significant distress, leaving the individual unable to integrate the pieces of their real vs. perceived experience of danger (Roach, 2013). Black men have been exposed to chronically traumatizing cultural experiences for generations. From slavery and lynch mobs to unyielding sociopolitical oppression, ongoing cultural trauma is an expected component of the Black male experience. Similar to individuals who are coping with traumas related to abuse, war, accidents etc., Black males have internalized a chronically hypervigilant posture as a way to manage the racism and discrimination associated with being a Black male. However, the Black male is oftentimes conflicted in his expression of hypervigilance due to the inherent fear and anxiety associated with this experience. As noted prior, Black masculinity is built on a foundation of toughness, aloofness, and emotional restriction. To admit to fearing for one's safety based on the color of one's skin or to acknowledge the underlying experience of anxiety related to chronic racism and discrimination would go against the traditional masculine ideology internalized by many Black men. Unable to reconcile the experience of fear and anxiety with the hypervigilance associated with exposure to cultural trauma, these men turn to aggression as a way to cope and protect themselves from future traumatization.

For example, let's examine a high school–aged Black male who has experienced multiple cultural traumas. This young man has witnessed a childhood friend who was unarmed shot by the police. In addition, he was regulated to special education classes at his school because he started falling behind and was told by his teacher that he should just focus on the things he can be good at, like sports. Furthermore, whenever the young man turns on the TV, he is inundated with messages highlighting how unsafe the word is for a Black male (e.g., number of homicides, unemployment rate, and the perpetuation of the scary Black man stereotype). Within this context, this Black male will experience chronic fear and anxiety about his ability to succeed in society and the dangers that he might be exposed to based on the color of his skin. To protect himself, this young man will assume a constant state of hypervigilance (an act first, ask questions later approach). However, as with many individuals who struggle with hypervigilant behavior, the Black male becomes unable to separate a real vs. perceived threat creating a scenario where every situation is viewed as threatening. In addition, similar to the priming theory discussed before, the use of overcompensating aggression becomes the most salient coping strategy for dealing with the threat of cultural traumas. Most hypervigilant behaviors are unconsciously produced and reinforced via a perception of success in avoiding a threat. With Black males, there is an additional layer to the perpetuation of aggressive behaviors that is influenced by the social conditioning of masculine over compensation via peer group norms.

"Man up!" This phrase quantifies the expectation that when a man is faced with a distressing situation, he must demonstrate an ability to master the situation within the confines of masculine ideology. When demonstrating this mastery or ability to man up, the individual will utilize the tools and coping skills most salient to his experience. As noted prior, the use of hyperaggression appears to be one of the coping skills most readily available for Black males. This phenomenon is due in part to the hypervigilance experienced based on the chronic exposure to racism and discrimination. However, the use of aggression is also consistently reinforced by the Black male's peer group.

Within the Black male's peer group, there is a strong endorsement for the use of aggressive behaviors. In order to gain acceptance, the Black male must be able to demonstrate that he can be aggressive and withstand the aggressive behaviors of others. In addition, the Black male learns that aggressive behaviors are the most respected solutions to problems. Someone challenges the individual verbally; he becomes obligated to use physical violence to rectify the situation. If a Black male does not engage in these behaviors, he risks losing his membership in the peer group as well as the use of aggressive behaviors being turned on him. For example, take a young Black male who is seeking acceptance into a particular peer group. In order to be a member of this group, the young man is told that he must accompany the group to find an individual who has disrespected the group by violating group norms (e.g., snitching). During the altercation, the young man is encouraged to hit the individual as a way to signify his membership and his adherence to the use of aggressive behaviors as a part of the peer group. Conflicted by seeking acceptance, the young man completes the task. As time passes, the young man continues to engage in aggressive behaviors within the peer group and begins to generalize the use of aggression outside of peer group activities (e.g., assaulting a teacher for giving him detention, yelling and pushing his mom for attempting to discipline him). One day, the young man is faced with a situation in which he has violated a peer group norm; to secure his membership, he is told that he must engage in increasingly aggressive behavior (e.g., robbery).

Thus a cycle is created where peer group norms dictate the use of aggressive behavior for respect and acceptance: → young Black male seeking to secure acceptance and respect engages in aggressive behaviors → aggressive behaviors become generalized to outside relationships → the young Black male receives rejection from outside relationships → he adheres more to peer group norms to secure acceptance in light of rejection → the peer group requires acts of increasingly aggressive behavior. This cycle leaves the Black male in the position of being compelled to engage in increasingly more aggressive behavior to gain acceptance and respect in the face of rejection from society as well as to prove he has the ability to man up. A last piece important to understanding the influence of aggression in Black male identity development is the concept of displaced aggression.

Underemployed, undereducated, and over-institutionalized, Black males represent a vulnerable segment of the population. These factors coupled with discriminatory experiences have left many Black men with underlying feelings of powerlessness and hopelessness. When individuals feel unable to affect change in systems or individuals that cause them distress, they will look to take out their feelings of anger and frustration on those who are peripherally related to the distress. This concept is called *displaced aggression*. According to Reijntjes et al. (2013), displaced aggression describes acts of aggression against individuals who were at the wrong place at the wrong time and serves as a channel for anger that cannot be directed at the source. Under the constant threat of imprisonment and consistent reminders of how they are not living up to the demands of traditional masculinity, many Black men have given up hope about their ability to change their situations. However, this lack of hope is coupled with a baseline of anger and frustration. Since Black men perceive that they are unable to directly confront popular culture and society with aggression, they displace their aggression onto the people they feel powerful against, other Black men.

For example, take a young Black male who has been in and out of the justice system. Marked as an "untouchable" for employment due to having a felony, the young man feels unable to take care of his family. Overwhelmed with the stress of trying to live up to his stereotypical responsibilities as a man, the young man can feel the anger and shame rising inside of him. As he is consistently met with barriers at every attempt to change his circumstances, the young man begins to develop chronic feelings of hopelessness and powerlessness. However, the underlying anger is still there and grows with increasing feelings of vulnerability. Perceiving that he does not have the ability to challenge the school system that failed him or the workforce that has shut him out, he turns his aggression inwards by displacing it onto other Black men. Angry about his circumstances and frustrated with the chronic feelings of hopelessness, he begins to view every action by another Black male as a challenge to the manhood denied to him by society. A scuffed shoe is an act of war. A name called, a reflection of his inability to thrive in a discriminatory society. In the end, the young man begins to internalize the beliefs that served as the basis for denying his Black masculinity and he hates himself and those that look like him as much as society has been taught to hate and fear him. This example highlights the concept of displaced aggression and how it is used by individuals (e.g., Black males) as a way to manage their feelings of aggression against systems or circumstances they feel powerless to change.

    This section has discussed the ways in which Black learn about aggression and its use. Due to the experience of multiple cultural traumas, many Black men have adopted a hypervigilant model of aggression to protect themselves from future traumatic events. In addition, looking for acceptance after facing rejection from society, many Black men turn to peer groups who endorse a posture of hyperaggression as a requirement for group membership. Lastly, coping with feelings of powerlessness and hopelessness, many Black men direct their aggression towards themselves through aggressive acts towards other Black men because they feel unable to challenge the systems that initially instilled the feelings of hopelessness. The last section of this chapter will explore how Black men can use the skill of assertiveness to adaptively cope with pressure from peer group norms and feelings of powerlessness when faced with challenging situations.

Assertiveness has been described as demonstrating self-assurance without being aggressive. Assertive individuals are able to effectively communicate their needs or issues in a way that doesn't disregard the experience of the other individual. Many Black men have learned to rely on aggression as a coping skill because it has been communicated via popular culture and their peer groups that it is the only tool that works and the only tool appropriate for Black men. Assertiveness is a skill that can be learned. The foundational components of being assertive include self-awareness, self-confidence, and clear communication. As discussed throughout this text, many of the challenges Black men face in regards to defining a coherent Black masculinity stem partly from unconscious processes and patterns of behavior that have been passed down through their families of origin (e.g., emotional restriction) and have been perpetuated in present-day society (e.g., aggression).

To develop the skill of assertiveness, Black men must develop a sense of self-awareness that acknowledges the generational transmission of behaviors and ways of thinking as well as an increased awareness of the stereotypical cultural box that has been designed for them. With self-awareness comes self-definition, where the Black male recognizes the sociohistorical reality but chooses to define his Black masculinity based on his perception and not the negative perception of Black men created by others. With increased self-awareness, Black men can feel more self-confident in who they are outside of the negative stereotypes forced upon them. Self-confidence contributes to recognizing the realities of the situation, but knowing that one has the strength and skills to master the circumstance or forge a new path. Lastly, an integrated knowledge of self combined with self-confidence can be complemented with an effective communication style, rounding out the assertive individual. Effective communication involves being direct (e.g., use of "I" statements), concise, and staying consistent with the intended message.

As a Black male develops his ability to be assertive, he will be less likely to rely on aggression as his only means of getting results. He will recognize that aggression is a long-standing coping skill passed down through families of origin and often serves as a requirement for acceptance (self-awareness). In addition, the Black male will observe that while some factors are outside of his influence, such as institutional discrimination (external control), he has infinite possibilities in managing his own behavior and thoughts and can find confidence in this experience. Lastly, by being able to clearly communicate his experience with racism, discrimination, and the perpetuation of negative stereotypes, he will be able to command a situation in a way that will gain him long-term respect and acceptance in a way that hyperaggressive behavior cannot fulfill.

Questions for Reflection

What lessons have you been taught about the use of aggression?

How do you feel the relationship between aggressive behavior and Black males is described in popular culture?

How does aggression fit into your definition of Black masculinity?

How has your family of origin and peer groups influenced your definition and use of aggression?

What challenges do you see in being assertive vs. being aggressive?

Reference

Lowe, S. M., Okubo, Y., & Reilly, M. F. (2012). A qualitative inquiry into racism, trauma, and coping: Implications for supporting victims of racism. *Professional Psychology: Research and Practice, 43*(3), 190–198.

Reijntes, A. et al. (2013). Too calloused to care: An experimental examination of factors influencing youths' displaced aggression against their peers. *Journal of Experimental Psychology: General, 142*(1), 28–33.

Roach, C. (2013). Shallow affect, no remorse: The shadow of trauma in the inner city. *Peace and conflict: Journal of Peace Psychology, 19*(2), 150–163.

Sprankle, E. L., End, C. M., & Bretz, M. N. (2012). Sexually degrading music videos and lyrics: Their effects on males' aggression and endorsement of rape myths and sexual stereotypes. *Journal of Media Psychology, 24*(1), 31–39.

Chapter 5

RACIAL/ETHNIC IDENITY: I AM WHATEVER I SAY I AM

Race and Ethnicity Overview

As the research on identity development has increased, a loss of clarity in demarcating between racial identity and ethnic identity has resulted (Worrell & Gardner, 2006). Neufeldt (1995) defined ethnicity as a description of a group of people having common customs and characteristics, such as dress, language, and food. Additionally, Neufeldt defined race as any of the different varieties of human beings distinguished by physical traits such as blood type, skin color, hair texture (1995). From a social science perspective, Phinney (1990) indicated that no consensus can be reached on the definitions of ethnic or racial identity. Phinney added that about two thirds of the literature on this topic didn't purport any type of explicit definition. One reason for the difficulty in quantifying the constructs of racial and ethnic identity may be that for individuals who identify with marginalized groups, they are unable to disentangle fully personal and social identities (Worrell & Gardner-Kitt, 2006).

For example, for African Americans the disentangling process may be particularly difficult because it requires reclaiming an identity that has been taken away by social injustices and negative historical experiences (Worrell & Gardner-Kitt, 2006). Based on this observation, most research examining racial attitudes and behaviors has focused on negative attitudes and behaviors, such as discrimination, about marginalized groups. (Phinney, Chavira, & Tate, 1992). Most researchers agree that race and ethnicity represent two distinct categories (Worrell & Gardner-Kitt, 2006). Additionally, it is important to note that there are more ethnic groups than racial groups (Phinney, 1990). For example, an individual can be racially identified as Black based on phenotypic characteristics such as skin color and texture of hair. However, ethnically this individual may identify with a number of different cultures, including Black American, African, Caribbean, or Jamaican. Based on this idea, there are several definitions of race and ethnicity posited in the literature and will be explored in the next section.

Defining Racial Identity

According to Phinney (2005), racial identity refers to an individual's physical appearance and the social meaning given to that appearance by society via historical events. This definition implies that racial identity is dually influenced by biological as well as social factors. For example, African Americans who were fairer skinned during the early 1900s would attempt, sometimes successfully, to pass for White individuals. During this time period, certain social characteristics in regards to intelligence, sexuality, aggressiveness, and morality were negatively associated with anyone who appeared biologically Black and darker skinned (Gates, 2004).

Worrell and Gardner-Kitt (2006) stated that racial identity describes a sense of group identity that is based on the individual's perception that he or she shared a common racial heritage with similar others. Racial identity represents a set of permanent biological characteristics that are categorized by such factors as skin color, hair texture, eye shape, and ancestral origin. These characteristics are quantified by population measures such as the United States Census, where individuals are grouped into limited categories, such as African American, Asian, or Caucasian. Utilizing this framework, racial-identity development focuses less on changing racial characteristics and more on integrating the individual's perceptions with social expectations of his or her racial group.

These definitions of racial identity have also influenced empirical research used to measure this construct. For example, Phinney and Ong (2007) found that the study of racial identity focused on responses to racism and the assessment of experiences related to internalized racism. For example, racial-identity studies may assess the participants' experience with racism and use this as a factor in regards to determining the level of influence these experiences have on their self-esteem. The samples for these studies focused on Black and White populations with college students. Ethnic identity, although oftentimes associated with racial identity, has distinct features of its own in regards to the components that comprise this construct and the influence they have on the individual's overarching sense of identity (Phinney, 1990).

Defining Ethnic Identity

According to Phinney (1990), the construct of ethnic identity explains how an individual draws on his or her ethnic heritage in the face of threats to his or her identity. Ethnic identity thus represents an internalization of the meaning associated with this membership (Phinney, 2005). Furthermore, the construct of ethnic identity is multifaceted and derives from social experiences over time. Worrell, Conyers, Mpofu, and Vandiver (2006) noted that ethnic identity is most salient in communities where multiple ethnic groups are in contact with one another. If the community is ethnically homogenous, then ethnic identity has less meaning within this context.

According to Phinney and Ong (2007), ethnic identity consists of several components, including self-categorization and labeling, commitment and attachment, exploration, ethnic behaviors, evaluation in group attitudes, values and beliefs, and salience. In defining these terms, self-categorization refers to identifying oneself as a member of a particular social group and is considered to be a basic element of group identity. Commitment and attachment refer to a strong attachment and personal involvement in a group. This is typically what is meant by the term ethnic identity. Exploration is defined as seeking information and experiences relevant to one's ethnicity. Exploration can thus include activities such as learning cultural practices and attending cultural events. Ethnic behaviors are considered to be the key aspect of ethnic identity and generally refer to the knowledge and use of an ethnic language. In-group attitudes typically include feeling comfortable with one's ethnicity and having positive feelings about one's group membership. Values and beliefs are seen as important indicators of one's closeness to the group. Lastly, salience or importance of ethnic identification has been shown to reflect the experience of ethnic minorities rather than members of the dominant majority (Phinney & Ong, 2007).

Ethnic identity represents a set of cultural norms, including or irrespective of racial characteristics, which have been integrated into the overall identity of the individual. For example, although an individual's continent of origin is Asia (his or her racial group), he or she may identify with a specific ethnic group (e.g., Nepali) that has its own cultural customs and traditions. Furthermore, the process of ethnic-identity development differs from racial-identity development in regards to an emphasis on the integration of cultural norms and the level of importance placed on his or her ethnic identity. Despite the differences between the constructs of race and ethnicity, they do share a number of similarities.

Similarities Between Race and Ethnicity

Phinney and Ong (2007) noted several similarities between race and ethnicity, including the development of a sense of belonging to a group, a dynamic process of learning about one's ethnic and racial group, a significant connection to cultural behaviors and values, and attitudes or beliefs towards one's own group. In addition, the authors indicated that both of the constructs of race and ethnicity vary in their importance and salience across times and context (Phinney & Ong, 2007). The process and variability of racial and ethnic identity development has been the focus of much of the identity development research. Phinney (2010) described this similarity in regards to the influence of race and ethnicity on the identity-development process. According to the author, the awareness of ethnic and racial difference is age dependent and the understanding of these differences changes systemically with age (Phinney, 2010). For example, children conceptualize the construct of ethnicity in a literal sense as defined by tangible concepts such as food, traditions, and languages. As the child's cognitive capacity for more abstract thinking matures, he or she develops a group consciousness. With this increased understanding, the individual begins to view the construct of ethnicity in terms of group cultural norms and values (Phinney, 2010). As a prelude to a more in-depth discussion of the influence of race and ethnic development on psychological well-being, the following paragraph will briefly highlight the literature in this area.

Race/Ethnicity and Psychological Well-being

According to Phinney (2005), positive outcomes in regards to psychological well-being have been found for individuals with a more developed ethnic identity compared to those who lack this understanding about the meaning of their ethnicity. In addition, in racial-identity–development research, low self-esteem has been shown to be related to the earliest stages of development, such as Pre-Encounter and Immersion/Emersion, whereas high self-esteem has been shown to be related to later stages of development (Parham & Helms, 1985). In regards to the convergence of race, ethnicity and gender differences, Phinney (1990) indicated that women demonstrate greater involvement in ethnic development than men. In addition, Parham and Helms (1985) found that African American men were more likely to endorse earlier stages of racial identity than African American women. However, Phinney, Chavira, and Tate (1992) noted that a strong sense of ethnic background was associated with a higher collective self-esteem in minority males.

African American Identity

Due to the rich heritage and culture of African people and individuals of the African Diaspora—defined as an individual whose continent of origin is Africa who has been dispersed throughout the world due to historical and societal factors—most African Americans identify strongly with their ethnic roots and culture. A study surveyed individual responses to questions concerning race, religion, politics, and American identity; the researchers found that 72% of African Americans stated that their racial identity was very important to them (Croll, 2007). In addition, 40% of the African Americans in the sample reported that they had a unified racial identity. Taken together, these results indicate that identifying with certain cultural mores are central to the self-concept of the African American identity. African Americans also possess the desire to integrate these self-concepts into a unified self-construct.

The following section will explore and discuss the literature that has examined the components of the African American identity. In addition, several models of African American identity development will be discussed, such as Cross's *Nigrescence* theory and Phinney's Three stage model of Ethnic Identity Formation. The literature will be examined and synthesized to highlight the pros and cons of each model in regards to their ability to accurately capture the African American identity through progressive stages of identity development. The following section will conclude with a discussion of the limited literature highlighting the influence of identity development in African Americans on the expression of psychological symptoms. Specifically, the section on African American identity will examine the literature discussing the influence of progressive stages of identity development in African American males and their relation to the development of psychological symptoms, such as anxious or depressive symptoms.

African American Identity Development Overview

Prior to the 1970s, most studies of Black identity development attempted to map the African American social-identity experience onto theories of White identity development or involved the comparison of Black and White scores on personality inventories (Cross, 1971). These studies did not consider factors specific to the African American identity experience such as racism, discrimination, and the lack of standardized samples for Blacks used for the personality inventories. According to Cross (1971), the omission in these studies contributed to African

Americans being associated with negative personality characteristics (e.g., dangerous or antisocial) and negatively stereotyped (e.g., scary Black man). However, Worrell et al. (2006) indicated that these studies were based on a limited sample of African American standardized research with no accurate description of a general theory of African American identity and its comprised constructs or significant information in relation to the convergence of racial identity and mental health relevant to the treatment and prevention of psychological symptoms in African Americans.

Since the 1970s, a more progressive analysis of the African American identity and its development has been the focus of several studies (Cross, 1971; Pierre & Mahalik, 2005; Phinney, 2007). The researchers sought to define the key features of the African American identity makeup. The theorists moved away from describing African American identity in terms of ego or personality variables, as emphasized by theorists such as Erik Erikson, to a focus on the development of the African American identity based on associating with a reference-group orientation such as ethnicity, gender, or sexual orientation (Helms, 1990; Phinney, 1989). Also, these theorists sought to describe how the various stages of development led to the creation of an identity.

In discussing African American identity development, Worrell et al. (2006) indicated that identity theorists make two assumptions in regards to this construct. First, theorists assume that universal profiles of Black racial identity exist across various populations of African Americans and that these attitudes and stages are relatively stable within the context of other cultural factors such as gender or socioeconomic status. Secondly, theorists assume that different racial-identity profiles are related to different patterns of cognitive, affective, and psychological functioning. The assumptions associated with differing patterns via racial identity profiles will serve as the backdrop for the discussion on African American identity as this manuscript highlights the empirical research and models in this area.

According to Kirscheinman and Meckerman (1991), the African American identity must accomplish two tasks: (a) assembling a positive sense of self, and (b) discrediting negative identities attributed to African American males and females. The latter task has been defined as *stereotype vulnerability* and is described as a need to consistently disavow group-based negative feedback (Spencer & Steele, 1992). With this concept in mind, Oyerman et al. (1995), proposed three core schemas to explain the purpose of the African American identity: (a) to make sense of the self as a group member; (b) to lend meaning and organization to current and historical racism, limited opportunities, and successes of African Americans; and (c) to organize self-relevant knowledge about personal effort and its meaning to an African American male or female. Based on a sample of undergraduates and previous research, Oyserman et al. (1995) found that in conjunction with the aforementioned schemas, the African American identity consists of three main components: a sense of community and embeddedness, awareness of racism, and individualized effort as an African American. A sense of community refers to a world view focusing on spiritualism and connectedness with the social environment. Awareness of racism implies the development of coping skills to address group marginalization by mainstream society. Lastly, individualized effort refers to the desire to obtain academic and occupational success.

In regards to African American males, Taylor (1991) stated that they have the added component of negotiating their identities by disconfirming the four d's: dangerous, deviant, dumb, and deprived. To address these issues, Majors and Billson (1993) stated that African American males have added an extra layer to their identity called the cool pose. The cool pose is defined as a ritualized form of masculinity that entails behaviors, scripts, physical posturing, and impression management (Majors & Billson, 1993). The goal of the cool pose is to deliver a message of pride, strength, and control in the face of seemingly insurmountable obstacles. The components of the cool pose include showing no emotion, fearlessness, aloofness, and displaying a "tough guy" persona. According to Majors and

Billson (1993), the cool pose is incorporated into the African American male identity to protect against the anxiety of second-class status and to hide feelings of self-doubt, insecurity, and inner turmoil.

A recent advancement that has been made in the literature in regards to the study of African American identity concerns the demarcation of the difference between racial identity and ethnic identity in this population. Additionally, there has been some research exploring how this dichotomy could influence the operationalization of identity constructs in African Americans (Cokley, 2005). Cokley (2005) indicated that many African American identity researchers use the terms ethnicity and race interchangeably. The author noted that there are important differences between ethnicity and race. For example, the author indicated that identity models are utilizing the construct of race when they describe reactions to societal oppression based on race. Furthermore, researchers are utilizing the construct of ethnicity when they describe the acquisition and maintenance of cultural characteristics such as religion, nationality, language, and ancestral history (Cokley, 2005). However, not all researchers have agreed on these proposed definitions of race and ethnicity.

Phinney's (1992) description of ethnicity involved three psychological aspects: culture, ethnic identity, and minority status. Culture indicates an individual's adherence to values, beliefs, and behaviors associated with his or her cultural group. Ethnic identity refers to the degree to which he or she identifies with his or her ethnic group. Lastly, minority status refers to the extent to which the individual has differential experiences and attitudes that are connected with having a minority status. According to Phinney (1992), the term minority status refers to racial identity as well, due to the fact that minority status is based on readily identifiable characteristics such as skin color and gender. Additionally, the attitudes connected with being a part of a minority group are largely influenced by experiencing racist behaviors and prejudicial attitudes. A component of racial-identity development is to challenge these behaviors and beliefs by developing more adaptive coping skills such as the inclusion of an Afrocentric or multiculturalist racial identity. Based on this definition of ethnicity, Phinney (1996) stated that ethnicity includes race and that these two constructs should be combined as an overarching construct.

Helms and Talleyrand (1997) argued against Phinney's concept of ethnicity and race characterizing a single construct. The authors stated that the term ethnicity has no meaning outside of its status as an alternative for racial classification. Furthermore, Helms and Talleyrand (1997) stated that the term race has a clear meaning as a designated racial category based on phenotype. The authors also indicated that in the literature, individuals are treated or studied based on belonging to a biologically defined racial group and the characteristics associated with that group. Lastly, as an argument for the distinction of race as a singular construct, the authors noted that advantageous or disadvantageous treatment occurs according to phenotypic characteristics, such as race, regardless of cultural socialization and ethnicity.

Based on the observation of race as a singular construct, the authors stated that the role that race plays in society is more salient than that of ethnicity. For example, if an individual came from South Africa to the United States, his or her experience would be different based on skin color. A White individual would be characterized ethnically as African American, but racially he or she would be described as White and would be afforded the privileges associated with that racial background. A Black individual from South Africa would also be characterized ethnically as African American, but racially he or she would be described as Black and subjected to the discrimination associated with this racial background. Although each individual's ethnic identity, South African, may be important to his or her experience, the way they are defined and the treatment they receive is based on racial characteristics. The previous example highlights Helms and Talleyrand's (1997) point that race and ethnicity are distinct constructs with differing influence on identity development.

Other African American identity-development researchers have sought to differentiate between ethnic identity and racial identity. Helms (1996) suggested that identity models describe a racial experience when people define the acquiring and maintenance of cultural characteristics, such as spiritual beliefs, music and art, and language. In addition, Helms stated that ethnicity refers to differences in nationality, ancestry, and culture that create a group identity based on personal and social meanings.

As noted previously, Phinney (1996) posited that ethnicity supersedes the construct of race. Parham (2002) took Phinney's ideology a step further and indicated that to develop a comprehensive understanding of African American identity requires a focus on an ethnic identity rooted in an Afrocentric worldview. The Afrocentric worldview thus serves as the foundation of African American identity and African cultural values. According to Cokley (2005), these cornerstone values of African American identity within the Afrocentric worldview include spiritualism, collectivism, communalism, and a belief in self-knowledge as the foundation for all knowledge.

Cokley (2005) conducted a study to investigate the differences between racial identity and ethnic identity in African Americans. The author found that a non-racialized ethnic identity was characterized by the endorsement of Afrocentric values, a strong ethnic identity, the negative endorsement of internalized racialism, and the absence of anti-White attitudes. In contrast, a racialized identity was found to be characterized by anti-White attitudes, beliefs about Afrocentrism, a belief in the natural ability of Blacks, a strong ethnic identity, and the negative endorsement of multiculturalist inclusive attitudes. These results indicated that in regards to the study of African American identity, racial identity and ethnic identity are two constructs with several separate identifying characteristics. Differentiating the level of identity is important in identity development research.

In summary, the study of African American identity has yielded several descriptions of what suggests a comprehensive picture of the cultural values, norms, and ideologies associated with this group of people. One important concept that all these descriptions have in common is their universal agreement in regards to the complexity of the African American experience. The African American experience has been significantly influenced by social factors, such as racism and discrimination, due to the minority status characteristic of this population. The following section will explore the African American identity models that have sought to quantify the convergence of societal conditions and racial identification, such as the Cross Nigrescence theory and Phinney's Three stage model of Ethnic Identity Formulation.

African American Identity Development Models

According to Oyersman et al. (1995), identity development serves two purposes: (a) it lends meaning and organization to experiences, such as thoughts, feelings, and actions; and (b) it motivates action by providing incentives, standards, plans, strategies and scripts for behavior. In regards to Black identity development, Majors and Billson (1993) added a third purpose of Black identity development as a protective factor against historical marginalization by mainstream society. The current section will elaborate on the main models used to describe the African American identity-development process.

Cross's Nigrescence Theory

During the colonial period of many African countries in the twentieth century, the Senegalese politician and poet Leopold Senghor encouraged people of the African continent to commence on a journey towards Nigrescence (French for turning Black), and seek to replace the negative attitudes associated with being Black with positive ones, according to Senghor (as citied in Worrell et al., 2006). According to Cross (1971), the African American journey towards Nigrescence can be traced back to two phases of Black historical events in the United States. The first phase consisted of the Civil Rights phase which, spanned from 1954 to

1965. The Civil Rights time period saw the passage of significant legislation, spurned by collective demonstrations in the Black community, which provided the opportunity for equal rights under the law for African Americans (Worrell et al., 2006). According to Cross (1994), the Civil Rights movement was driven by self-concepts that affirmed the Black individual's connection with the cultural and national identity of the United States.

The second phase was coined the Black consciousness phase and occurred from 1965 to the late 1970s. The Black Consciousness phase was characterized by a high level of militancy in the Black community and a significant emphasis on racial autonomy and between-group differences. These phases culminated in the establishment of the Contemporary Black Social Movement. The Contemporary Black Social Movement spanned the 1980s and 1990s. The movement introduced an explosion of Black literature, music, and popular culture, such as hip hop. In addition, the movement was defined by such events as the Million Man March and Anti-Apartheid demonstrations. Cross (1971), influenced by the progression of these movements in African American culture, sought to create a comprehensive spectrum of Black identity development that would capture the African American individual's progression from a period of racial self-hatred, as evidenced by studies of Black identity development prior to the 1970s, to a period of racial acceptance and integration. The following section will explore the evolution of Cross's Nigrescence theory over the past three decades. In addition, the subsequent section will examine Cross's original theory as well as its revised and expanded forms. Furthermore, the literature that supports and criticizes Nigrescence theory will be discussed.

Cross's original nigrescence theory. Cross's original Nigrescence theory was proposed in 1971. According to Vandiver (2001), Cross's model of Black identity development was conceptualized as the process of an African American individual accepting and affirming a Black identity within the context of American Nationalism by moving from a stage of Black racial self-hatred to a stage of Black racial self-acceptance. Worrell et al.

(2006) also indicated that this process consisted of transitioning from a pro-White assimilationist position, accepting only White values and attitudes, to a pro-Black internalized stance, incorporating Black cultural values and attitudes into one's identity. According to Cross (1994), the original model consisted of five stages: Pre-encounter, Encounter, Immersion–Emersion, Internalization, and Internalization–Commitment. Each of these stages was indicated to be characterized by different racial attitudes, each of which consisted of distinct cognitive and affective elements (Vandiver, 2001).

The first stage, Pre-Encounter, described an African American individual whose identity is governed by the values of the dominant culture. These individuals have internalized a pro-White identity and an anti-Black stance. Individuals in the Pre-Encounter stage were hypothesized to be self-hating and to demonstrate low self-esteem and poorer psychological functioning (Cross, 1971). The second stage, Encounter, consists of a Black individual experiencing an affective laden event, or series of events, that causes him or her to question his or her beliefs about the role of race in mainstream society (Cross, 1994). These racially charged events cause the individual to reexamine his or her belief system concerning race and to reevaluate his or her racial identity within this context. According to Cross (1994), the next stage, Immersion–Emersion, represents a volatile two-pronged transition from the individual's old racial identity to a new self-concept.

During the Immersion component, individuals immerse themselves in African American culture to the point of developing ethnocentric beliefs (Vandiver, 2001). The immersion the individual experiences permeates all facets of the individual's life and can manifest itself in regards to choice of clothing, political activism, name change, hair style, and choice of literature and art. These individuals develop a strong pro-Black identity and adopt a strong anti-White identity, which emphasizes the dichotomous thinking evident during this stage, where everything Black is good and everything White is bad (Cross, 1994). According to Parham and Helms (1985), the all-or-nothing mode of thinking may be due in part to the individual's hypersensitivity to the negative perceptions of African Americans in the dominant culture. The individual in turn attempts to compensate for this overemphasis by idealizing Blackness and denigrating Whiteness.

The Emersion component of Immersion–Emersion is characterized by a racial identity reevaluation process where the individual becomes emotionally stable and begins to reexamine his or her experiences and racial identity (Cross, 1994). According to Vandiver (2001), the achievement of a balance in affect and cognition results in the abandonment of anti-White beliefs and progression into the Internalization stage. The Internalization stage is characterized by the intellectual and emotional acceptance of the individual being Black (Cross, 1971). The individual is able to integrate several self-concepts into a coherent identity. However, the individual's Black racial identity serves as the foundation on which these self-concepts are established. The individual in the Internalization stage has achieved a sense of inner security in regards to his or her Blackness, which contributes to ideological flexibility and a decline in intense anti-White beliefs.

The last stage, Internalization-Commitment, is characterized by a further progression of Black self-acceptance (Cross, 1971). The progression of Black self-acceptance is represented behaviorally by the individual becoming involved in social activism centered around social change and civil rights issues. In regards to psychological functioning, Vandiver (2001) indicated that progression from the Pre-Encounter stage to the Internalization stage reflects a movement from psychological maladjustment to positive psychological well-being. Worrell et al. (2006) revised the Nigrescence theory in 1991 to reflect adjustments to these criticisms and empirical findings (Cross, 1991). The following paragraph will discuss the changes made in the model and how these changes impacted Cross's Nigrescence theory.

Revised nigrescence theory. According to Vandiver (2001), the revised model was an accumulation of Cross's analysis of the empirical literature concerning Nigrescence theory as well as an evolution in his own thinking about Black identity development. The revised theory contained some of the tenets central to the original theory, but significant changes were made in a number of areas, including changes to the Pre-Encounter and Internalization stages, placing greater emphasis on demarcating between an individual's reference group orientation and personal identity, and the introduction of the concept of race salience and its influence on Black identity development (Vandiver, 2001). Cross (1991) stated that the revised model also addressed changes in thinking in regards to the existence of multiple identities within each stage, and the reevaluation of the link between Black identity development and self-esteem. These changes will be explored in the following section as well as their overall influence on the general Nigrescence theory.

As indicated previously, significant changes were made to the Pre-Encounter stage in the revised Nigrescence model (Cross, 1991). The original Pre-Encounter stage was thought to capture an individual who had adopted a strong Pro-White identity and had internalized an anti-Black stance (Cross, 1971). The individual who endorsed an anti-Black stance was believed to be suffering from low self-esteem and psychological maladjustment because of the denigration of their African American heritage. However, the literature did not support this theoretical concept, indicating a weak correlation between pro-White attitudes and self-esteem (Worrell, Cross, & Vandiver, 2001). To account for this new evidence, Cross (1991) used the term *race salience*, rather than Pro-White, to indicate the importance of race in a particular individual's life, and as a general factor in his or her identity development. According to Vandiver (2001), race salience refers to the level of importance or significance that race plays in influencing a person's worldview. The race salience concept can be divided across two measurable dimensions: degree of importance and the direction of the valence. These dimensions indicate that in regards to race salience, an individual can rank race as lower or higher and report a positive or negative valence, or degree of attraction or aversion.

To adjust for the weak correlation found between pro-White identity and self-esteem, Cross (1991) stated that acceptance of an American nationalist perspective and the rejection of Black culture was not indicative of one's identity in the Pre-Encounter stage. Instead, the Pre-Encounter stage can be subdivided into two identities. The first identity was called Pre-Encounter Assimilation. This identity characterizes the individual's adoption of a pro-American nationalist or mainstream identity. Race is not viewed as important in this stage. According to Vandiver (2001), individuals who demonstrate a Pre-Encounter Assimilation identity are not necessarily Anti-Black in nature. Instead these individuals exhibit a low race salience with a neutral valence, or lack of awareness of a racial identity. Contrarily, the second identity within the Pre-Encounter stage was the Pre-Encounter anti-Black identity. The Pre-Encounter anti-Black identity describes an individual who hates Blacks and Black culture, as well as being Black, and exhibits a high negative racial salience towards African Americans (Cross, 1991).

According to Cross (1991), two components form the basis of the Anti-Black identity: miseducation and racial self-hatred. Miseducation refers to the idea that Blacks hold negative stereotypical beliefs about being Black that they have learned from their environment, such as being lazy or unintelligent. Cross took this idea from the work of noted social commentator Carter G. Woodson. Woodson (1933) posited that African Americans, through the depictions of Black people in mainstream, had been conditioned to see themselves as inferior and dependent upon members of the dominant culture. Woodson claimed that this conditioning stemmed from a "miseducation of the Negro." In Cross's Nigrescence theory, individuals had taken this miseducation so far as not only hating their African American reference group, but also in regards to hating themselves for being a member of this reference group. The intense self-hate for the African American provided the second basis for the Anti-Black identity.

According to Vandiver (2001), Black self-hating individuals incorporate the negative stereotypes they have learned about Blacks into their own personal identity. Because of this, individuals in the Anti-Black stage have an intense hatred of Blacks and in turn hate themselves because they are Black. Cross (1991) posited that this self-hatred caused the low levels of self-esteem in Pre-Encounter individuals. He indicated that per the empirical evidence, low self-esteem was not linked to the formation of a Pro-White identity, as demonstrated by the Assimilation identity, but by harboring an Anti-Black identity. Cross (1991) stated that this phenomenon occurred because these individuals have developed an intense Black self-hatred which stemmed from the incorporation of negative stereotypes into their personal identity, culminating in the presentation of low self-esteem.

In regards to the Encounter stage, Cross (1991) emphasized the fact that the relevance of the stage stems from the developmental influence on racial identity change. Cross (1991) further stated that because the Encounter stage can be a single event or a number of smaller emotionally tinged episodes, it is highly personal and not as easily categorized as the other stages of the Nigrescence theory due to the fluidity in this period of development. Cross (1991) indicated that the Immersion–Emersion stage represented the vortex of psychological Nigrescence. The vortex aspect of the Immersion–Emersion stage did not change in the revised model. However, Cross (1991) stated that what changed in this theory was an increased emphasis on a dual-vision nature of this stage in regards to the world and societal values.

In general, these two visions consisted of ideas that were on the same continuum of racial beliefs where everything Black is seen as good and everything White is seen as bad. To address this dichotomy, Cross (1991) redefined the role of Black Nationalism. In the original Immersion–Emersion stage, Black nationalism had been used to define a series of intense Afrocentric beliefs (Cross, 1971). However, in the revised model, Black nationalism was depicted as a positive internalization of being Black with pride and self-acceptance. The intense Afrocentric beliefs were seen as separate from the ideals of Black Nationalism. With the Black nationalism concept in mind, Cross (1991) delineated two identities involved in the Immersion–Emersion stage: intense Black involvement and anti-White.

According to Cross (1991), Intense Black involvement refers to an immersion in the culture of Blackness that is characterized by the excessive embracing of everything that is conceptualized as Black. Cross (1991) indicated several benefits to the assumption of this identity. For example, due to an increased desire to learn more about Black culture, these individuals may be more well-informed. However, the exploration of Blackness is fueled by intense feelings of rage, guilt, and anxiety, which can be destructive in nature and hard to control. These feelings stem from the individuals' effort to reconcile their new awareness of Blackness with the worldview that has been presented to them by society (Cross, 1991). Vandiver (2001), indicated that these individuals feel anger because they have been deceived by society. In addition, they harbor guilt because they feel that they have betrayed their race by accepting unquestionably the views of Blackness held by mainstream society. Cross (1991) also highlighted two additional behavioral indicators for this identity. First, individuals in the intense Black involvement identity take a very hard stance toward other African Americans who are in the Pre-Encounter or Internalization stage. These individuals are unable to distinguish between these two stages and see both as representing Pro-White attitudes. In addition, these individuals develop Anti-White attitudes that can manifest in a variety of social settings, including overt and covert racism. These Anti-White attitudes represent the second component of the revised Immersion–Emersion stage (Cross, 1991).

During the Anti-White component of the original Immersion process, individuals demonstrated a tendency to denigrate White individuals and White culture (Cross, 1971). These attitudes emerge as a consequence of the intense immersion of the individual into the ideology of Blackness. Cross (1991) indicated in his revised model that an overt expression of contempt for White culture was less likely to occur compared to the racial tensions that existed during the era of the Civil Rights Movement. From a behavioral and cognitive standpoint, Cross (1991) stated that anti-White sentiments existed in the Immersion stage as passive-aggressive tendencies, such as daydreams and fantasies about harm coming to White individuals. Cross (1991) also suggested that Anti-White attitudes can become a permanent fixture of an individual's Black racial identity, separate from the intense Black involvement immersion identity. When individuals in the Immersion–Emersion stage are able to bring their heightened emotionality in regards to racial issues under control, they progress to the Internalization stage.

In the original model, Internalization was broken up into stages: Internalization and Internalization–Commitment (Cross, 1971). During the Internalization stage, Cross (1971) indicated that individuals put aside the guilt and rage of the Immersion stage and accept themselves in their Blackness without idealizing it. The Internalization–Commitment stage was marked by the individual seeking out regular involvement in diverse organizations. In the revised model, Cross stated that based on empirical evidence, few significant differences existed between the psychology of Blacks at the Internalization or Internalization–Commitment stage (1991). Because of this observation, these two stages were combined into one Internalization stage. Vandiver (2001) also suggested that the Internalization stage was no longer synonymous with a universal acceptance of relationships among diverse cultural groups. Instead, the level of cultural acceptance occurred on a continuum where internalized Blacks differ in their acceptance of members from diverse cultural groups. These observations culminated in the inclusion of three identities under the Internalization stage: Black Nationalist, Biculturalist, and Multiculturalist (Vandiver, 2001).

The common thread between each one of these identities is Black self-acceptance and reflects the main tenet of the Internalization stage. As indicated by Vandiver (2001), Black Nationalism can be defined as a focus on Black empowerment, economic dependence, and a greater awareness of Black culture and beliefs. In the literature on Black Nationalism, two views were described that influenced the description of this identity: separatist and inclusion (Vandiver, 2001). The separatist view stems from the ideology that individuals of African descent needed to migrate back to Africa or that African Americans needed to establish a separate nation within the United States.

The second view was inclusion and indicated that Black Nationalism emphasized a strong Black racial consciousness in tandem within the American educational, political, and cultural system (Worrell, Cross, & Vandiver, 2001). Cross (1991) incorporated these ideas of Black Nationalism in the Black Nationalist identity and stated that for these individuals, being Black is the only salient identity and is demonstrated through social and political activism that empowers the Black community. The Biculturalist identity describes the original intent of the Internalization stage. As noted before, Black individuals in the original Internalization stage were thought to be open to other cultures and worldviews while opposing racism and oppression (Cross, 1971). The Internalization worldview was tempered by individuals internalizing a sense of Black self-acceptance that was influenced by a humanist perspective. Cross (1991) noted that outside of the individual's new ability to negotiate various identities of race and nationality, other aspects of culture were not addressed, such as gender, ableism, and heterosexism. Cross (1991) sought to address this absence in the Nigrescence theory through the formation of the Biculturalist identity. According to Vandiver et al. (2001), the internalized Bicultural identity describes an individual who has achieved self-acceptance of being both Black and American. Thus a person in this stage is able to incorporate two cultural identities within his or her internalized cultural framework.

The last identity within the revised Internalization stage of the Nigrescence theory was an internalized Multicultural identity. Here, being Black is salient, but at least two other cultural identities are afforded equal weight within the dynamics of the individual's cultural identity (Vandiver, 2001). For example, an African American individual can emphasize being Black as part of their identity as well as being male or female or adhering to certain religious traditions. In addition, individuals with this set of identity characteristics are viewed as being accepting of others from diverse racial backgrounds.

In summary, the transition from Cross's original Nigrescence theory to the revised Nigrescence theory was marked by changes in several areas (Cross, 1991; Vandiver, 2001; Worrell, Cross, & Vandiver, 2001). First, Cross (1991) stated that multiple racial identities existed within each stage. The inclusion of multiple racial identities was in contrast to Cross's original hypothesis that a discrete set of unitary behaviors could describe an individual at each stage of identity development (Cross, 1971). Also, the relationship between Black identity development and self-esteem was reevaluated. Low self-esteem was posited to be caused by a sense of Black self-hatred as opposed to the internalization of pro-White attitudes (Cross, 1991). Lastly, the Internalization stage was reduced from two stages to one, and a range of identity pathways were described. In 2001, the Nigrescence theory underwent another revision to its current form as the expanded Nigrescence theory (Vandiver, 2001; Worrell, Cross, & Vandiver, 2001). The following paragraph will explore these changes as well as highlight their influence on the general model of Black identity development.

Expanded nigrescence theory. According to Worrell (2008), the expanded Nigrescence model retained the name of the stages from the previous model, Pre-Encounter, Immersion–Emersion, and Internalization. However, instead of being conceptualized as developmental stages, they were described as identity clusters that influenced that individual's worldview. The Pre–Encounter identity clusters include racial attitudes in which being Black is given low or negative salience. Immersion–Emersion identity clusters include highly salient attitudes towards Blacks and Whites. The attitudes present in this identity cluster are emotionally volatile because they stem from exposure to racism and discrimination (Vandiver et al., 2001). According to Worrell et al. (2001), the expanded model consists of nine Nigrescence attitudes: three Pre-Encounter attitudes (Assimilation, Miseducation, and Self-Hatred), two Immersion–Emersion attitudes (Intense Black Involvement and Anti-White), and four Internalization attitudes (Nationalist, Biculturalist, Multiculturalist Racial, and Multiculturalist Inclusive). Three of these identity clusters are unique to the expanded model: Pre-Encounter Self-Hatred identity, Multiculturalist Racial, and Multiculturalist Inclusive.

In the original Pre-Encounter stage of the Nigrescence theory, individuals were believed to represent a unidimensional construct of Black self-hatred (Cross, 1971). The intense self-hatred, evidenced by the internalization of a pro-White identity, was hypothesized to be associated with lower levels of self-esteem in these individuals. However, Cross (1991) found that individuals could internalize Pro-White worldviews and not exhibit low self-esteem. In his revised theory, Cross (1991) reconceptualized this stage and divided it into two stages: Anti-Black and Assimilation. It was indicated that in this revision, Assimilation, or pro-White, attitudes were not associated with low self-esteem. Instead, anti-Black attitudes that implied a hatred for Black culture, without necessarily incorporating White worldviews, were the basis for the feelings of low self-esteem indicated in this population (Cross, 1991).

In the expanded Nigrescence theory model, Vandiver et al. (2001) indicated that the current empirical literature supported the presence of three Pre-Encounter Attitudes: Assimilation, Miseducation, and Self-hatred. The Assimilation attitude was a carryover from the revised model and referred to the internalization of pro-White attitudes. The Miseducation attitude was formerly known as the Anti-Black attitude and referred to the perceived source of these anti-Black attitudes, including an internalization of negative stereotypes and beliefs about African Americans. The Self-hatred attitude was separated from the Anti-Black attitude because empirical research indicated that African

Americans can have negative stereotypes about African Americans without hating themselves (Worrell, Cross, & Vandiver, 2001). Vandiver et al. (2001) indicated that the results were inconclusive in regards to the influence of racial self-hatred on self-esteem and required further study in future research.

As noted previously, two attitudes were added to the expanded Nigrescence theory Internalization attitude: Multiculturalist Racial and Multiculturalist Inclusive (Vandiver et al., 2001). In the revised model of the Nigrescence theory, the Internalization stage was divided into three racial attitudes: Black Nationalism, Biculturalist, and Multiculturalist. Black Nationalism refers to a pro-Black, non-racist orientation that is focused exclusively on the construct of race. The Biculturalist attitude refers to the individual's ability to incorporate a sense of positive Black self-acceptance as well as the internalization of another cultural identity such as nationality or gender. The Multiculturalist attitude was associated with a positive Black self-acceptance and the incorporation of two or more salient cultural identities (Worrell, Cross, & Vandiver, 2001). The expanded model suggested that based on empirical research (Vandiver et al., 2001), the Multiculturalist attitude could be broken down into two additional attitudes: Multiculturalist Racial and Multiculturalist Inclusive. The Multiculturalist Racial attitude refers to an individual assuming a multiculturalist orientation in regards to cultural concepts centered around race (Worrell et al., 2006). However, these individuals do not incorporate various other cultural components outside of race, such as gender and sexual orientation. The Multiculturalist Inclusive attitude describes individuals that have moved beyond the cultural confines of race and seek to include multiple cultural identities into their identity formation (Worrell et al., 2006).

In summary, the expanded model of the Nigrescence theory provided several significant changes to the general theory (Vandiver et al., 2001; Vandiver et al., 2006; Worrell, Cross, & Vandiver, 2001). Although the names of the various components were retained from the original model, they were no longer conceptualized as developmental stages but as identity clusters that influence one's worldview (Worrell, Cross, & Vandiver, 2001). In addition, individuals are indicated to have some of all of the levels of attitudes in the Nigrescence theory. The inclusion of a multilevel endorsement of racial attitudes is in sharp contrast to the previous versions of the theory which suggested that individuals fit into specific stages based on characteristics discrete to each component of the theory.

Three Stage Model of Ethnic Identity Formulation

Phinney (1990) defined ethnic identity as a feeling of belonging to one's identified ethnic group, a clear understanding of the meaning of one's membership in this group, and demonstrating positive attitudes towards this group, indicated by a familiarity with the ethnic group's history, culture, and participation in its associated practices. The Three Stage Model of Ethnic Identity Development stemmed from a dearth in the literature concerning the psychological relationship between ethnic minority group members and their identified ethnic group (Phinney, 1990). The following paragraph will explore the development of this model and its corresponding components.

According to Phinney (2010), identity is formed as a result of actions and choices made by the individual in response to developmental progression and the cultural demands in the community he or she lives in. Phinney's conceptualization of identity serves as the basis for the three stage model of ethnic identity development and is rooted in the ego identity model of Erik Erikson and the personal identity development of James Marcia. As indicated by Phinney (2007), Erikson referred to identity as a subjective feeling of sameness and continuity that provides the individual with a stable sense of self and guidance for key choices in his or her life. Within Erikson's ego identity model, identity develops over time through a process of reflection and observation. Achieved identity in the ego identity development model consists of childhood identifications, individual interests and talents, and contextual opportunities (Phinney, 2007).

According to the Phinney (2007), Marcia conceptualized identity formation as involving the exploration of identity issues and specific behaviors associated with each identity status. Marcia's model consisted of four identity statuses: Identity diffusion, Identity foreclosure, Moratorium, and Achieved identity. Identity diffusion describes individuals who have not engaged in either exploration or commitment. Identity foreclosure indicates individuals who have made an identity commitment without exploring their identity fully. The moratorium period refers to individuals who are in the process of exploring an identity without making a commitment. Lastly, individuals who have explored significant identity issues and have made an identity commitment describe the achieved identity status (Phinney, 2007).

Based on these models, Phinney (2007) indicated that ethnic identity refers to a sense of self, but that it differs from the ego or personal identity because it involves a shared sense of identity with others belonging to the same ethnic group. In addition, according to Phinney (1990), the process of ethnic identity formation involves the construction over time of one's sense of self as a member of a social group. Based on this ideology, Phinney (1990) developed the three stage model of ethnic identity formulation to capture this process and the varying levels of understanding associated with greater achieved identity. The three stages of the model include unexamined ethnic identity, ethnic identity search, and achieved ethnic identity. Unexamined ethnic identity refers to an individual who has unexamined positive or negative views of their ethnic groups. Ethnic identity search describes an individual who has begun a search into what it means to be a member of the ethnic group. Lastly, achieved ethnic identity represents individuals who have explored their ethnic group membership and have a clear understanding of the meaning of ethnicity in their life (Phinney, 1989). According to Phinney (1990), the perception of one's ethnicity is central to positive psychological functioning for those ethnic minorities who are subjected to a marginalized status by dominant cultures. For example, utilizing Phinney's model, Phinney, Chavira, and Tate (1992) found that Hispanics with a stronger ethnic identity had developed more positive strategies for discrimination leading to a more resistant ethnic identity and sense of self-esteem. However, a solid ethnic identity is difficult to accomplish due to these groups being poorly represented in areas such as the media or in politics. Phinney (2007) indicated that the formation of an ethnic identity provides an avenue for understanding how to be resilient in the face of constant threats to one's group identity.

Racial and Ethnic Identity and Mental Health

As noted previously, racial-identity development has been posited as consisting of an individual's attempt to reconcile the racism and discrimination he or she experiences based on biological characteristics (Cross, 1991). In contrast, ethnic identity means to reconcile one's identification within a group that has a marginalized status compared to a dominant ethnic group (Phinney, 1990). At the center of these distinct developmental processes is the development of coping skills, such as an advanced racial identity, or the development of an integrated ethnic identity, to cope with race-related stress. In anticipation of the discussion examining the convergence of racial and ethnic identity and mental health, the following paragraph will explore the concept of race-related stress and its seminal influence on psychological distress in minority individuals.

Race-related stress. According to Harrell (2000), race-related stress refers to "a race-related transaction between individuals and their environment that emerge from racially charged events and that tax or exceed the individuals collective resources or threatens his/her wellbeing" (p.45). Utsey, Lanier, Williams, Bolden, and Lee (2006) also noted that race-related stress occurs as the result of both acute and chronic encounters with racism and discrimination.

Hobfoll (2001) indicated that racial stress arises in regards to experiences when an individual's resources are threatened with loss, the individual loses his or her resources, or the individual fails to gain needed resources after significant effort. Several authors have suggested that race-related stress, which is exacerbated by racial discrimination, can negatively affect the psychological well-being of African Americans (Cross, 1991; Utsey et al., 2006). Hobfoll (2001) noted that racism can lead to stressful conditions that influence psychological well-being, including exposure to negative stereotypes that threaten an individual's psychological resources, persistent and systemic experiences of racism that result in the actual loss of psychological resources, and the undermining of significant psychological resource investment on the part of the individual.

Unfortunately, racial discrimination is a common phenomenon in the Black community and many of these individuals are forced daily to negotiate this discrimination in their lives. According to Sellers and Shelton (2005), racial discrimination can be both blatant, such as the use of a racial slur, or covert, such as being followed around in a shopping mall. Kessler, Mickelson, and Willams (1999), conducted a national survey with 3,032 individuals living in the United States that assessed the national prevalence of major lifetime perceived discrimination and day-to-day perceived discrimination. The results from the survey indicated that 60% or more of African American adults encounter racial discrimination in their daily lives. Furthermore, the authors found that perceived discrimination was positively associated with the experience of mental health issues in African Americans.

According to Utsey, Giesbecht, Hook, and Stanard (2008), race-related stress has important consequences for the psychological health of African Americans. In a study of 127 predominantly female elderly African Americans, Utsey, Payne, Jackson, and Jones (2002) examined the relationship between race-related stress and quality of life. The authors found that race-related stress was a significant predictor of psychological health in this population (Utsey, Payne, Jackson, & Jones, 2002).

Experiences of racism or discrimination have also being found to be related to lower levels of self-esteem and increased depressive symptoms (Wakefield & Hudley, 2007). Landrine and Klonoff (1996) conducted a study with 153 African Americans, using the Schedule of Racist Events, to measure the influence of race-related stress on psychological well-being. The authors found that race-related stress was related to symptoms of anxiety, depression, and somatization in African American males aged 15–70 (Landrine & Klonoff, 1996). The results from this study support the hypothesis of the current study in regards to the experience of race-related stress, when not buffered by racial or ethnic identity development, being associated with psychological symptoms in African American males.

Pierre and Mahalik (2005) surveyed 130 from a college and community sample using the RIAS, African Self-Consciousness scale, and the Symptom Checklist-90. The authors compared the experience of Pre-Encounter, Immersion, and Internalization racial identity attitudes to scores on the SCL-90 Global Severity Index (GSI). The authors noted that race-related stress appears to significantly affect African American males in a number of ways, including a shortened life expectancy, and higher incidences of stroke, high blood pressure, and hypertension. Additionally, the authors found that those individuals with Pre-Encounter and Immersion Attitudes reported greater psychological distress and lower self-esteem than those individuals with Internalization attitudes. Pierre and Mahalik's (2005) study was one of a few studies in the literature that examined the convergence of racial identity and psychological well-being in African American males.

The literature has noted that the development of coping strategies to deal with racism is important in regards to overcoming the effects of race-related stress (Utsey et al., 2006). Utsey, Giesbecht, Hook, and Stanard (2008) indicated that specific coping strategies include eliminating or modifying the source of the stress, altering the meaning of the discriminatory event, or regulating the emotional response associated with event or action.

One process that can influence the development of these coping skills, potentially leading to a reduction in race-related stress and ultimately an improvement in psychological well-being, is the development of a more advanced racial identity or the integration of a more positive and coherent ethnic identity. Although it has been indicated in previous studies that there are a number of pathways to the presentation of psychological symptoms in African Americans (Hammock, 2003), the current study will focus on ethnic and racial identity development. The emphasis on ethnic- and racial-identity development is based on the observation that several studies of these constructs have demonstrated significant variance related to ethnic and racial identity and their ability to moderate psychological symptoms in African Americans.

Several studies have suggested a link between ethnic and racial identity and the development of psychological symptoms (Parham & Helms, 1985; Pyant & Yanico, 1991; Whittaker & Neville, 2010). Specifically, the literature has indicated that those individuals with an integrated ethnic identity or the endorsement of more progressive racial attitudes demonstrate fewer psychological symptoms; in comparison to those who report a less integrated ethnic identity or the endorsement of less progressive racial attitudes. The literature on this topic has suggested that the inclusion of an integrated ethnic identity or the endorsement of progressive racial attitudes may serve as a buffer against the effects of race-related stress through the promotion of cultural awareness and the maintenance of adaptive coping skills. The following section will discuss the literature in regards to the convergence of racial and ethnic identity and mental health. In addition, the following section will examine the current literature highlighting the influence of racial and ethnic identity on mental health in African American males.

Racial identity and mental health. According to Cross, Parham, and Helms (1991), the development of a Black racial identity serves three functions: providing protection against psychological injury, achieving meaning in one's definition of Blackness, and developing a multicultural perspective that serves as a bridge between one's Blackness and the greater community.

The authors also noted that the positive expression of racial identity in African Americans can increase cultural awareness and promote self-esteem in ways that buffer against the effects of daily racial discrimination (Cross, Parham, & Helms, 1991). Specifically, the literature has indicated that those individuals who identify with minority groups and have a high level of racial identity may be better able to cope with racial discrimination than individuals with a lower level of racial identity (Pyant & Yanico, 1991).

Racism and discrimination are a constant part of the African American experience due to this group's status as a marginalized minority (Kessler, Mickelson, & Williams, 1999). Racial identity development is posited to be the individual's reconciliation of the negative experiences associated with his or her racial group and attempt to develop a positive racial concept (Cross, 1991). According to the current identity-development literature, this process may moderate the effects of racism and discrimination, via race-related stress, on the psychological well-being of African Americans (Utsey et al., 2006). Specifically, the literature indicates that a more advanced racial identity, such as the Internalization racial attitude, may serve as a buffer against these negative effects (Pyant & Yanico, 1991; Whittaker & Neville, 2010).

Ethnic identity and mental health. Ethnic identity has been described as the acquisition and maintenance of cultural characteristics, such as ancestral history, language, religion, and nationality, that inform personal and social meanings of group identity (Cokley, 2005). Although the construct of ethnic identity has been used interchangeably with racial identity, the current literature has indicated that these two constructs represent two different phenomena. Cokley (2005) conducted a study highlighting the difference between ethnic and racial identity.

The author found that a distinction existed between ethnic identity and racial identity. This distinction was quantified in the terms Nonracialized Ethnic Identity and a Racialized Ethnic Identity. A Non-Racialized Ethnic Identity refers to a strong ethnic identity, negative endorsement of internalized racism, and the absence of anti-White attitudes. A Racialized Ethnic Identity refers to anti-White attitudes, beliefs about Afrocentrism, a belief in the natural ability of Blacks, and the negative endorsement of multiculturalist-inclusive attitudes. Although an African American individual can have both a strong ethnic and racial identity, an individual can endorse more Afrocentric beliefs, which are an indicator of an African American racial identity, without the development of an ethnic identity. The influence of endorsing more Afrocentric beliefs is explicit in biracial individuals who may endorse African American cultural beliefs, or ethnic identity, while incorporating a multiculturalist's attitude and the negative endorsement of internalized racism, a Non-Racialized Ethnic Identity.

According to Phinney (1990), the construct of ethnic identity provides an avenue for understanding the need for an individual to draw on their ethnic heritage in the face of threats to one's identity. Ethnic identity represents an internalization of the meaning associated with this membership (Phinney, 2005). Furthermore, ethnic identity represents a set of cultural norms, including or irrespective of racial characteristics, which have been integrated into the overall identity of the individual. The process of ethnic identity development differs from racial identity development in regards to an emphasis on the integration of cultural norms and the level of importance placed on his or her ethnic identity. Based on these differences, ethnic identity may have a similar yet distinct influence on psychological well-being to racial identity. However, in regards to African American males, results from these studies that examine ethnic identity are difficult to generalize to this population due to a lack of focus and poor sampling. The following paragraphs will explore the literature regarding the influence of ethnic identity on psychological well-being.

According to Wakefield and Hudley (2007), members of ethnic minority groups in a hierarchal multiethnic society have the difficult task of reconciling the extent to which they will maintain a unique group identity, identifying with characteristics of the dominant society to improve their chances for success, and identifying with other minorities in a marginalized status. Similar to racial identity, ethnic-identity development can have a significant effect on the psychological well-being of ethnic minority groups by buffering the influence of race-related stress (Wakefield & Hudley, 2007). Furthermore, as noted by Phinney and Kohatsu (1997), those individuals with a more advanced sense of ethnic identity exhibit better psychological adjustment than those in the earlier stages of their ethnic identity development.

Because of their marginalized status, many ethnic groups are forced to reconcile the extent to which they identify with their ethnic group or take on the characteristics of the dominant ethnic culture (Wakefield & Hudley, 2007). The literature has indicated that the development of a positive ethnic identity can serve as a buffer during this process as the individual attempts to examine the negative beliefs associated with his or her ethnic group (Gray-Little & Hafdahl, 2000). In particular, it has been noted in the literature that those individuals with a more advanced ethnic identity may demonstrate more buffering ability than those with a less advanced ethnic identity (Choi, Harachi, Gillmore, & Catalano, 2006).

Psychological Distress and Racial identity development

According to Mirowsky and Ross (2003), psychological distress can be defined as "the unpleasant subjective state of depression and anxiety which has both emotional and physiological manifestations" (p. 8). Furthermore, Watkins and Jefferson (2012) noted that these manifestations can take on an additional level of specificity called mood and malaise. Mood describes an individual's feelings (e.g., sadness, fear) and malaise highlights an individual's physiological state and behavioral anchors associated with the experience of feelings (e.g., cold sweats, headaches). Sellers, Bonham, Neighbors, and Arell (2009), indicate that African American men experience disproportionately higher levels of psychological distress due to their exposure to a greater frequency and severity of psychological stress compared to men from other racial groups (e.g., discrimination, low SES).

The literature has indicated that the development of coping strategies is important in regards to overcoming the effects of psychological distress (Watkins & Jefferson, 2012). Specific coping skills include regulating the emotional response associated with the stress, eliminating or modifying the source of the stress, developing an adaptive social network, and fostering a sense of meaning in life (e.g., racial identity development). Potentially at the center of this process is the development of a more advanced racial identity. A more advanced racial identity has been demonstrated to be correlated with fewer psychological symptoms in comparison to those who report a less advanced identity.

Cross, Parham, and Helms (1991) suggested that the development of a Black identity serves the functions of providing protection against psychological injury, achieving meaning in one's definition of Blackness and developing a multicultural perspective that serves as a bridge between one's Blackness and the greater community. Individuals with a dominant Pre-Encounter Self-Hatred attitude have not achieved these attitudes. Instead, these individuals have developed an intense Black self-hatred that stems from the incorporation of negative stereotypes. Furthermore, the experience of racial self-hatred significantly influenced their experience of psychological distress.

The Immersion–Emersion Anti-White status describes individuals with highly salient negative attitudes towards Whites that stem from exposure to racism and discrimination (Vandiver et al., 2001). These individuals attempt to reject all mainstream cultural influences and immerse themselves into Black culture, such as by wearing African clothing and joining Black organizations (Worrell et al., 2001). Findings from previous studies indicate that the endorsement of an Anti-White racial attitude is associated with somatic complaints, interpersonal difficulties, hostility, paranoia, and global psychological distress. However, individuals with a dominant anti-White status do not report the same level of severity of psychological symptoms as individuals endorsing a self-hatred racial attitude. The differential outcome between these racial identity statutes suggests that the combination of racial self-hatred for oneself and one's identified racial group may have more of an influence on the experience of psychological distress, and poorer coping abilities for racism and discrimination, than anti-White attitudes.

In regards to the influence of a more advanced racial identity development, the findings of previous studies provide support for a negative relationship between the Internalization Multiculturalist Inclusive racial attitude and psychological distress. Individuals who endorse the Multiculturalist Inclusive racial attitude have incorporated a sense of positive Black self-acceptance as well as the internalization of multiple cultural identities such as nationality or gender (Worrell, Cross, & Vandiver, 2001). These individuals have moved beyond the cultural confines of race as they move into this next stage of their identity formation (Worrell et al., 2006).

Psychological Distress and Ethnic Identity Development

In the literature, ethnic identity refers to a shared sense of identity with others belonging to the same ethnic group (Phinney, 2007). The process of developing an ethnic identity involves the construction over time of one's sense of self as a member of a social group and the individual's attitudes associated with membership in the group (Phinney, 1990). Models of ethnic-identity development suggest that individual's progress from a period of possessing an unexamined ethnic identity, through searching for what it means to be a member of his or her identified ethnic group, to achieving a clear understanding of the meaning of his or her ethnic background in their lives (Phinney, 1989). According to Phinney (1990), the perception of one's ethnicity is central to positive psychological functioning for those ethnic minorities who are marginalized by the dominant culture. Similar to racial-identity development, ethnic identity has been shown to influence psychological well-being via serving as a buffer against the effects of discrimination. Phinney (2007) indicated that the formation of a positive ethnic identity provides an avenue for understanding how to be resilient in the face of constant threats to one's group identity.

Previous studies have found that ethnic identity is strongly associated with the experience of psychological distress in African American males. Specifically, the findings from these studies indicated that the stronger the individual's ethnic identity, in regards to integration and positive endorsement, the lower psychological distress they reported. Phinney (2010) indicated that identity is formed as a result of actions and choices made by the individual in response to development progression and cultural demands of the community. For ethnic minorities, including African American males, ethnic identity may serve as a buffer from the psychological distress associated with deleterious experiences stemming from a marginalized status.

According to Phinney, Chavira, and Tate (1992), a stronger ethnic identity is associated with the development of more positive strategies for coping with the psychological distress associated with discrimination and racism. Specifically, Phinney (2007) indicated that for minority individuals, ethnic identity provides an avenue for understanding of how to be resilient in the face of constant threats to one's group identity. African American males with a stronger ethnic identity have developed more adaptive coping skills to handle the constant threats to their identities as African Americans compared to those African American males with a less developed ethnic identity. Furthermore, a stronger ethnic identity contributes significantly to the lessening in the report of psychological distress for these individuals.

Questions for Reflection

What does it mean for you to be a member of your race?

How do you define Blackness?

How does society define Blackness?

How were you taught about your racial heritage? What lessons did you learn?

What is your ethnic heritage? What components (e.g., dress, food, and religious activities) contribute to this heritage?

How do you feel that a racial knowledge of self has contributed to your psychological well-being?

Reference

American Psychiatric Association. (1994). *Diagnostic and statistical manual of mental disorders* (4th ed.). Washington, DC.

Cross, W. (1971). The Negro to Black conversion experience. *Black World.* 13–27.

Cross, W. (1991). *Shades of Black: Diversity in African American identity.* Philadelphia: Temple University Press. 499–521.

Cross, W., Parham, T., & Helms, J. (1991). Stages of Black identity development: Nigrescence models. In R. L. Jones (Ed.), *Black Psychology* (3rd ed., pp. 319–338). New York: Harper & Row.

Hammack, P. (2003). Toward a unified theory of depression among urban African American youth: Integrating socioecologic, cognitive, family stress and biopsychosocial perspectives. *Journal of Black Psychology, 29,* 187–209.

Helms, J. (1986). Expanding racial identity theory to cover counseling process. *Journal of Counseling Psychology. 33*(1), 62–64.

Helms, J. & Carter, R. (1991). Relationships of White and Black racial identity attitudes and demographics similarity to counselor preferences. *Journal of Counseling Psychology, 38*(4), 446–457.

Hobfoll, S. (2001). The influence of culture, community, and the nested-self in the stress process: Advancing conservations of resources theory. *Applied Psychology: An International Review, 50*, 337–370.

Kessler, R., Mickelson, K., & Williams, D. (1999). The prevalence, distribution, and mental health correlates of perceived discrimination in the United States. *Journal of Health and Social Behavior, 40*, 208–230.

Kirschenman, J. & Neckerman, K. (1991). "We'd love to hire them, but…": The meaning of race for employers. In C. Jencks and P. E. Peterson (Eds.), *The urban underclass* (203–232). Washington, DC: Brookings.

Landrine, H. & Klonoff, E. (1996). The Schedule of racist events: A measure of racial discrimination and a study of its negative physical and mental health consequences. *Journal of Black Psychology, 22*, 144–168.

Majors, R. & Billson, J. (1992). *Cool pose: The dilemmas of Black manhood in America.* New York, NY: Touchstone.

Ong, A., Fuller-Rowell, T. & Phinney, J. (2010). Measurement of ethnic identity: Recurrent and emergent Issues. *Identity: An International Journal of Theory and Research, 10*, 39–49.

Oyserman, D., Gant, L., & Ager, J. (1995). A socially contextualized model of African American identity: Possible selves and school persistence. *Journal of Personality and Social Psychology, 69*(6), 1216–1232.

Parham, T. & Helms, J. (1981). The influence of student's racial identity attitudes on preferences for counselor race. *Journal of Counseling Psychology, 28*, 143–147.

Parham, T. & Helms, J. (1985). Attitudes of racial identity and self-esteem of Black students: An exploratory investigation. *Journal of College Student Personnel, 28*, 143–147.

Pierre, M. & Mahalik, J. (2005). Examining African self-consciousness and Black racial identity as predictors of Black men's psychological well being. *Cultural Diversity and Ethnic Minority Psychology, 11*(1), 28–40.

Phinney, J. (1989). Stages of ethnic identity development in minority group adolescents. *Journal of Early Adolescence, 9*, 34–49.

Phinney, J. (1990). Ethnic identity in adolescents and adults: Review of research. *Psychological Bulletin, 108*(3), 499–514.

Phinney, J. (1992). The multigroup ethnic identity measure. A new scale for use with diverse groups. *Journal of Adolescent Research, 7*, 156–176.

Phinney, J. (2005). Ethnic identity in late modern times: A response to Rattansi and Phoenix. *Identity: An International Journal of Theory and Research, 5*(2), 187–194.

Phinney, J. (2010). Understanding development in cultural contexts: How do we deal with the complexity? *Journal of Human Development, 53*, 33–38.

Phinney, J., Chavira, V. & Tate, J. (1992). The effect of ethnic threat on ethnic self-concept and own group ratings. *Journal of Social Psychology, 133*(4), 469–478.

Phinney, J. & Kohutsa, E. (1997). Ethnic and racial identity and mental health. In J. Schulenberg et al. (Eds.), *Health risks and developmental transitions during adolescence* (pp. 420–443). New York, NY: Cambridge University Press.

Phinney, J. & Ong, A. (2007). Conceptualization and measurement of ethnic identity: Current status and feature directions. *Journal of Counseling Psychology, 54*(3), 271–281.

Pyant, C. & Yanico, B. (1991). Relationship of racial identity and gender role attitudes to Black women's psychological well being. *Journal of Counseling Psychology, 38*(3), 315–322.

Sellers, R. & Shelton, J. (2003). The role of racial identity in perceived racial discrimination. *Journal of Personality and Social Psychology, 84*(5), 1079–1092.

Taylor, R. (1991). Poverty and adolescent Black males: The subculture of disengagement. In P. B. Edelman and J. Lander (Eds.), *Adolescence and poverty: Challenge for the 1990's* (pp. 139–162). Washington, DC: Center for National Poway Press.

Utsey, S. et al. (2002). Effect of ethnic group membership on ethnic identity, race-related stress, and quality of life. *Cultural Diversity and Ethnic Minority Psychology*, 8(4), 366–377.

Utsey, S., Chae, M., Brown, C., & Kelly, D. (2002). Effect of ethnic group membership on ethnic identity, race-related stress, and quality of life. *Journal of Cultural Diversity and Ethnic Minority Psychology*, 8(4), 366–377.

Utsey, S. & Constantine, M. (2008). Mediating and moderating effects of racism-related stress on the relation between poverty-related risk factors and subjective well-being in a community sample of African Americans. *Journal of Loss and Trauma*, 13, 186–204.

Utsey, S., Giesbrecht, N., Hook, J., & Stanard, P. (2008). Cultural, sociofamilial, and psychological resources that inhibit psychological distress in African Americans exposed to stressful life events and race-related stress. *Journal of Counseling Psychology*, 55(1), 49–62.

Utsey, S., Hook, J., & Standard, P. (2007). A re-examination of cultural factors that mitigate risk and promote resilience in relation to African American suicide: A review of the literature and recommendations for future research. *Journal of Death Studies*, 31, 399–416.

Utsey, S., Lanier, Y., Williams, O., Bolden, M., & Lee, A. (2006). Moderator effects of cognitive ability and social support on the relation between race-related stress and quality of life in a community sample of Black

Americans. *Journal of Cultural Diversity and Ethnic Minority Psychology, 12*(2), 334–346.

Vandiver, B. et al. (2001). Cross's Nigrescence model: From theory to scale to theory. *Journal of Multicultural Counseling and Development, 29*, 174–200.

Whittaker, V. & Neville, H. (2010). Examining the relation between racial identity attitude clusters and psychological health outcomes in African American college students. *Journal of Black Psychology, 36*(4), 383–409.

Worrell, F., Conyers, L., Mpofu, E., & Vandiver, B. (2006). Multigroup ethnic identity measure scores in a sample of adolescents from Zimbabwe. *Identity: An International Journal of Theory and Research, 6*(1), 35–59.

Worrell, F., & Gardner-Kitt, D. (2006). The relationship between racial and ethnic identity in Black adolescents: The Cross racial identity scale and the multigroup ethnic identity measure. *Identity: An International Journal of Theory and Research, 6*(4), 293–315.

BLACK MALE IDENTITY DEVELOPMENT SUMMARY

The intergenerational transmission of trauma has significantly impacted the experience of the Black male. Trauma-related behaviors have been developed as a way to protect Black men from the effects of slavery and chronic racism and discrimination. These trauma-related behaviors and ways of thinking have communicated messages of hopelessness and despair. Furthermore, they have manifested in the form of shame, guilt, rage, poor attachment, silence, and the development of confusing unspoken rules in families. At the individual level, trauma-related behaviors and ways of thinking appear as pseudo post-traumatic stress symptoms such as chronic reliving of the trauma, hypervigilance, and emotional numbing. Black masculinity represents a cultural encapsulation of these behaviors in the form of hyperaggression and alexithymia.

The development of Black manhood is a consciousness-raising process through which Black males seek to integrate sociohistorical and economically influenced expectations of masculinity. This process is significantly affected by contextual factors such as family of origin, peer groups, prison culture, and the media. Within this context, the development of a hypermasculine identity (e.g., hyperaggression, emotional restriction) stems from a reactionary attempt to create an alternative masculine identity in the face of chronic efforts to denigrate Black manhood.

In regards to emotional restriction, an alexithymic mode of thinking has been passed down from generation to generation of Black men to help manage the chronic experience of racism and discrimination. However, several problems have arisen due to the experience of alexithymia in Black males. First, the art of keeping them guessing has been turned inward in the form of the underdevelopment of emotional awareness. Secondly, through the social learning process and the internalization of a traditional masculine ideology, many Black men have become disconnected from their own emotional selves. As noted previously, this disconnection can contribute to the perception of an external locus of control (feelings of hopelessness about one's situation), the development of a passive coping style for emotionally charged situations, impulsive behavior in a desire to rid oneself of disagreeable emotional states, and chronic feelings of anxiety and anger that manifest as hostility towards oneself and others.

Furthermore, due to the experience of multiple cultural traumas, many Black men have adopted a hypervigilant model of aggression to protect themselves from future traumatic events. In addition, looking for acceptance after facing rejection from society, many Black men turn to peer groups who endorse a posture of hyperaggression as a requirement for group membership. Coping with feelings of powerlessness and hopelessness, many Black men direct their aggression towards themselves through aggressive acts towards other Black men. This happens because they feel unable to challenge the systems that initially instilled the feelings of hopelessness.

Lastly, in regards to Black men and mental health, racial- and ethnic-identity development can serve as a buffer for the experience of psychological distress related to racism and discrimination. Specifically, the endorsement of a more advanced racial identity has been found to serve as a buffer for psychological distress. This advanced racial identity is evidenced by achieving meaning in one's definition of Black and developing a multicultural perspective that serves as a bridge between one's Blackness and the greater community. In addition, a more integrated ethnic identity has also been shown to be a buffer for the experience of psychological distress. An integrated ethnic identity provides an avenue for an increased understanding of how to be resilient in the face of constant threats to one's group identity. African American males with a stronger ethnic identity have developed more adaptive coping skills to handle the constant threats to their identities. The combination of a more advanced racial identity integrated ethnic identity can facilitate the development of adaptive coping skills. These coping skills are developed through self-awareness and the endorsement of positive traits associated with one's race or ethnic group. With the development of these coping skills, Black males are able to internalize an alternative masculinity. This alternative masculinity acknowledges the sociohistorical ramifications of chronic racism and discrimination while highlighting the need for self-acceptance and self-definition.

BLACK MALE IDENTITY AND CLINICAL IMPLICATIONS FOR MENTAL HEALTH PROFESSIONALS

In the wake of the recent shootings of Black males such as Trayvon Martin and Oscar Grant, Black males presenting signs of mental illness may indicate concerns related to the experience of racism and discrimination (Fischer & Shaw, 1999). Discussing the effects of racism and discrimination with ethnic minorities in a clinical setting can be a difficult subject to navigate. However, studies have suggested that the clinician's willingness to engage this discussion can be beneficial (Elligan & Utsey, 1999; Sue & Sue, 2008). One area to consider when discussing racism and discrimination with a Black male client is their racial identity development. The following discussion will explore the concept of identity development and how it can influence a clinical conversation about racism and discrimination with this population. Furthermore, practical suggestions for discussing this subject based on Black males' racial-identity development will be provided.

In the midst of the social paradigm shift that occurred during the 1960s, Dr. William Cross developed a model of Black racial identity development that highlighted a progression from a lack of racial identity awareness or racial self-hatred (Pre-Encounter) to a hypervigilant sense of racial pride (Immersion–Emersion) to an internalized Multiculturalist or Afrocentric racial identity (Internalization). The process of racial identity development can be significantly influenced by the experience of racism and discrimination (Cross, 1991; Cross, Parham, & Helms, 1991). Based on the Cross model, the following recommendations are suggested for discussing the experience of racism and discrimination with Black male clients:

- **Pre-encounter status:** Black males endorsing this status will be largely unaware of the influence that their skin color has when it comes to the experience of discrimination and racism (Cross, 1991; Cross, Parham, & Helms, 1991). Exploration of this subject can exacerbate feelings of low self-esteem and anxiety and challenge their belief about experiencing differential treatment from other members of their race. When working with these Black males, it may benefit the client to help them navigate conflicts related to the experience of racism and discrimination through an appropriate reeducation process and by modeling positive attitudes towards cultural diversity (Sue & Sue, 2008).

- **Immersion–Emersion status:** Black males endorsing this status will strongly identify with issues of racism and discrimination (Cross, 1991; Cross, Parham, & Helms, 1991). In discussing the Black male's experience in this status, it may benefit the client to validate the negative influence that racism and discrimination has had in their lives. Furthermore, these clients are generally receptive to conversations that are action oriented and focus on the external change of racially oppressive systems (Elligan & Utsey, 1999; Sue & Sue, 2008).

- **Internalization:** Black males endorsing this status have developed an inner sense of security concerning their racial identity via the internalization of Afrocentric beliefs or a multiculturalist perspective (Cross, 1991; Cross, Parham, & Helms, 1991). In discussing issues of racism and discrimination with these individuals, they will typically acknowledge the reality of their experience with this issue. However, they may respond best to an action-oriented conversation aimed at societal change (Sue & Sue, 2008).

The tragic shooting deaths of Black men like Trayvon Martin has brought to the forefront that racism and discrimination are still a chronic part of the Black male experience. These events have highlighted the need for more dialogue concerning the experience of racism and discrimination by Black males. Clinicians must be willing and prepared to engage in this conversation with our Black male clients, with the intent of providing a safe space to explore this issue, its effect on racial identity, and what actions can be taken on the part of the client.

Reference

Cross, W. (1991). *Shades of Black: Diversity in African American identity.* Philadelphia, PA: Temple University Press. 499–521.

Cross, W., Parham, T., & Helms, J. (1991). Stages of Black identity development: Nigrescence models. In R. L. Jones (Ed.) *Black Psychology* (3rd ed., pp. 319–338). New York, NY: Harper & Row.

Elligan, D. & Utsey, S. (1999). Utility of an African centered support group for African American men confronting societal racism and oppression. *Journal of Cultural Diversity and Ethnic Minority Psychology, 5*(2), 156–165.

Fischer, A. & Shaw, C. (1999) African Americans' mental health and perceptions of racist discrimination: The moderating effects of racial socialization experiences and self-esteem. *Journal of Counseling Psychology, 46*(3), 395–407.

Sue, D.W., & Sue, D. (2008). *Counseling the culturally diverse: Theory and practice (5th ed.).* New York, NY: John Wiley & Sons

BLACK MALES AND DEPRESSION: SLIENT FUSTRATION

Men in America are expected to project characteristics of strength, individuality, autonomy, dominance, stoicism, and physical aggression. For Black males, identifying with and fulfilling these roles has been a challenge that oftentimes they have been unable to meet. One explanation may be that Black males oftentimes receive conflicted messages about Black masculinity from mainstream society and the Black community. On one hand, in mainstream society, Black males are often portrayed in a negative light (i.e. overly aggressive, sexually promiscuous, lazy, unmotivated). However, in the Black community, Black men are expected to live up to the three P's: Priest, Provider, and Protector. Depression in Black males may stem from this conflict in the form of a failed attempt to reconcile these two images or views into one successful individual. This failed attempt is further compounded by the fact that in general men are more likely to rely on themselves, to withdraw socially, and try to talk themselves out of feeling depressed. So what has happened is that we have a number of Black males (especially between the ages of 18–24) who, due to societal limitations in regards to finances and education, are unable to fulfill the expectations bestowed upon them. This causes these individuals to experience a chronic feeling of silent frustration.

Silent frustration highlights the exhaustion of resources to combat the chronic experience of racism and discrimination. Underlying this frustration are feelings of shame and guilt for not feeling able to fulfill their community's expectations as a Black man and feeling powerless against the negative stereotypes and expectations from society. This silent frustration evolves in phases that are influenced by constraints created by masculine ideology (e.g., restricted emotional expression, dependence on anger and aggression, the *John Henryism* effect). First, Black males are exposed to, and develop a heightened awareness of, racism and discrimination. Black men are more likely to report racially discriminatory events, with most quantified as *microaggressions*, which are brief verbal, behavioral, racially motivated slights that occur on a daily basis. For example, an individual telling a Black man, "Oh, you speak so well," implying that his use of proper English is not the norm for Black individuals. Black men seek to actively cope with this experience by doing what they have been taught in their community: "Work twice as hard to get half as much." This coping strategy has been defined as John Henryism. John Henryism is an active coping style that highlights the individual's belief in being able to influence their circumstances through hard work and determination. However, as with any coping strategy, John Henryism has its limits, leading to the second phase, anger and rage.

Feeling unable to influence their surroundings, Black men develop feelings of rage and anger towards these institutions (e.g., workplace, educational setting). These feelings create conflict within the Black male because of the conundrum of being angry at something that he feels he cannot change or influence. This rage then moves from the institution, to his community, and then ultimately within himself. Unable to verbalize the underlying feelings of shame and guilt (due to a restricted emotionality) this rage manifests as acts of violence shattering his interpersonal relationships and support systems within his community. Isolated and alone, the Black male develops feelings of hopelessness and powerlessness because of the constellation of emotions he is experiencing (shame, rage, and guilt) and the perceived lack of adaptive outlet for their expression and processing. With their coping resources exhausted and feeling isolated from their support systems, these Black men are regulated to suffering in silence, frustrated with their experience of racism and discrimination, and their perceived inability to effectively manage this conflict.

To help manage the silent frustration many Black men experience, the therapist must be willing to address several things.

First, an honest conversation should be conducted that validates the very real experience of racism and discrimination that Black men endure. Within the therapeutic setting, the therapist must be mindful of not falling into the trap of perpetuating the same microaggression that these individuals experience on a daily basis that will facilitate an expectation of trust and a willingness to understand. Secondly, Black men must be given the emotional language to voice the underlying feelings of shame and guilt because of their perceived inability to meet the expectations of adhering to a traditional masculine ideology. Third, the Black male and the therapist should collaboratively develop adaptive ways that he can feel empowered in regard to influencing his circumstances and environment (e.g., starting a non-profit, organizing a rally, starting a letter campaign, joining a mentorship program). Fourth, the Black male should be encouraged to develop a network of trust. This network of trust would consist of individuals with whom he feels comfortable communicating his frustrations concerning the racism and discrimination associated with being a Black male. The network would serve the purpose of keeping the individual from suffering in silent frustration alone. Lastly, *psychoeducation* should be provided that highlights the effects of racism and discrimination; its impact on feelings of shame, guilt, and rage; and their combined impact on experiencing hopelessness and powerlessness.

CLINCAL INTERVENTIONS SECTION

INTRODUCTION

Having explored Black masculinity and the various components that contribute to its development, this section offers a variety of interventions that can be used by helping professionals. This section offers only a small fraction of the possible interventions that can used with Black males and challenges related to Black male–identity development. Specifically, this section highlights interventions that can be used to address the experience of intergenerational trauma in families, alexithymia, aggression, and racial identity development. These interventions are not curative in isolation, but can facilitate an insightful discussion in a variety of settings (e.g., therapy, school, youth programs) that can contribute to the adoption of a positive Black masculinity.

Alexithymia

Emotion Identification Game

Treatment Modality: Individual

Goals
- Learn to identify various emotional states.
- Facilitate discussion concerning what emotions are more or less difficult to express.
- Improve emotional vocabulary to define emotional states.
- Facilitate discussion of how to identity emotional states in others.

Materials
- Faces with assorted feelings such as happy, sad, angry, frustrated, relaxed, bored, embarrassed, and anxious.
- Cutouts with feeling words to match faces.
- Tape.
- Markers.

Description
Hang up a feeling face on a board and ask the participant to match an emotion with a face. As each emotion is guessed, hang the emotion word with the corresponding feeling face. If an incorrect guess is made, ask for additional information about why they made their guess (e.g., "How do you know this person is . . . ?" "What type of face do you make when you feel . . . ?" "What about their face makes them look like they are feeling . . . ?"

The therapist can facilitate the participant's experience of the activity by using the following questions or statements:
- Which emotion is hard for you to express?
- Tell me about a time when you felt (mad, sad, happy, etc).

- What type of emotions do you see expressed in your family?
- Who is someone that you look up to? How do they handle their emotions?

Feelings Bingo

Treatment Modality: Group

Goals
- Learn to identify various feelings words.
- Hands on practice of using feeling words.
- Facilitate discussion concerning what emotions are more or less difficult to express.
- Improve emotional vocabulary to define emotional states.

Materials
- Bingo Cards (see appendix)
- Bingo Prizes (e.g., candy, small toys)

Description
Participants play the Feelings Bingo game with regular Bingo rules (e.g., five horizontal, vertical, or diagonal signals a winner). To expand the game and move past recognition to description, additional prizes can be awarded for describing the feeling as it is called out.

The therapist can facilitate the participant's experience of the activity by using the following questions:
- If I didn't know you, how would I know you were feeling . . . ?
- How do you know when your parents/caregivers are feeling?
- When was the last time you felt . . . ?
- If you saw that someone was feeling . . . how would you try to help them?

Emotions Charades

Treatment Modality: Group, Family

Goals
- Discuss the physical experience of emotions.
- Develop skill of identifying emotions in others.
- Learn to develop various emotional states.

Materials
None needed

Description
Participants take turns acting out various emotions, and other group members try to guess what emotion the participant is imitating. The acting out portion can involve anything from facial expressions (frowning, smiling), to body movements (clenching fists) to a combination of both for more complex emotions (e.g., being embarrassed).

The therapist can facilitate the participant's experience of the activity by using the following questions:
- What emotion was the hardest/easiest to identify?
- What emotion was hardest/easiest for you to express?
- Is it easier to guess your own feelings or the feelings of others?
- How would your expression of the emotion in the game be different from that of the participant who acted it out?

How Well Do You Know....

Treatment Modality: Family

Goals
- Facilitate discussion among family members of unique expression of feelings among individual members.
- Identify triggers for various feelings in family members.
- Facilitate a discussion among family members about the norms of what emotions are expressed in family system.
- Strategize adaptive ways or the continuance of adaptive ways to cope with challenging emotions with family members.

Materials
Marker
White Board

Description
This is a family emotion-identification game designed to highlight how emotions are learned in the family, what are the rules about emotional expression in the family, and the family member's ability to predicate how certain family members will emotionally respond to hypothetical situations. Individual family members are interviewed briefly to give their respective emotional reactions to an event. During the intervention, family members attempt to guess how their family member would feel and how they would express this emotion based on a scenario. Family members then discuss how accurate they were in their guess and what this might mean for actual events that may occur in the family system. This intervention can be used in a game format by assigning points based on correct answers.

The therapist can facilitate the participant's experience of the activity by using the following questions:

- What does that mean to you that your family was correct/incorrect about what your emotional experience would be?
- Are there other situations where you feel like your emotions were not heard or misinterpreted?
- How could your family validate your emotional experience?
- How does this activity highlight some of the rules about emotions and emotional expression in your family?

Generational Trauma

Family Genogram

Treatment Modality: Family

Goals
- Explore underlying traumas or significant events that have implicitly impacted the current family system.
- Highlight the reproduction of relational patterns in the family system across generations.
- Begin the process of discussing how to change negative patterns in the family system.

Materials
- Markers
- Pencils
- One large sheet of paper

Description
This is a family activity designed to highlight patterns of trauma in the family as well as facilitate a discussion of how these patterns have influenced the family's current dynamics. Using a large piece of paper and some markers, family members start with their current family unit (ages, significant events, relationship dynamics), include extended family (e.g., aunts, uncles, cousins) noting significant events, and move up to include prior generations (grandparents, great grandparents, etc.). Basic symbols for the genogram include the following: square for male, circle for female, horizontal line connection for married, a line with two slanted lines for divorced, a line with one slanted line for separated, an "X" in the square or circle for deceased, a squiggle line for a conflicting relationship, and a dashed line for a distant relationship.

The therapist can facilitate the participant's experience of the activity by using the following questions:

- What are some of the significant events that have occurred in your family?
- What traditions or ways of doing things have been passed down through your family?
- Who started these traditions? Why or under what circumstances?
- How does your family handle negative or challenging circumstances?
- Where did this coping style come from?

Family Story

Treatment Modality: Family

Goals
- Increase understanding of family dynamics via a shared narrative.
- Highlight events that have influenced the development of the family narrative.
- Begin the process of developing a new narrative that integrates a new understanding of patterns of familial trauma and the family's resources and strengths.

Materials
- Markers
- Pencils
- Large sheet of paper

Description
This activity will help the family tell their story. As the family's story unfolds, the therapist can point out significant "chapters" or pivotal events that have influenced the family's story and how they tell it. The therapist can expand on this story by highlighting how the family narrative has been passed down through the generations and the themes that have been consistently demonstrated in the family system. The therapist can work collaboratively with the family to integrate the various aspects of their story to create a more coherent narrative that includes a different understanding of the family dynamics.

The therapist can facilitate the participant's experience of the activity by using the following questions:
- What would be the title of your family's story?
- What are some chapters in your family's story?
- Who started your family's narrative?

- How has this narrative been passed down through your family?
- What are some themes present in your family's story?
- What do these themes tell you about your family?

Aggression

Conflict-Resolution Skills (Stop, Think, Question, Resolve)

Treatment Modality: Individual, Group

Goals
- Highlight the difference between assertiveness and aggression.
- Gain insight into how the way one thinks influences how they identify acts of perceived aggression.
- Discuss the physical symptoms and cognitive underpinnings of anger.
- Identify coping skills for anger.
- Discuss barriers to adaptive conflict resolution.
- Explore and role play conflict resolution skills.

Materials
- Markers
- Large sheet paper
- Note cards

Description

This activity will help participants improve their adaptive conflict resolution skills. The activity is broken into three phases. In the first phase, participants discuss the concept of anger, the difference between anger and aggression, and recognizing the cognitive, emotional, and physical cues for anger. In the second phase, participants discuss the Stop, Think, and Question method to conflict resolution. In the Stop step, participants are taught to recognize their warning signs for anger (e.g., clenched fist, heavy breathing) and to implement coping skills of varying intensity (e.g., squeezing a stress ball to mindful breathing to taking a time out) to provide a brief second for rational processes to kick in. In the Think step, participants are taught to differentiate between what they perceive and what they see in the situation that has made them angry. In the Question step, participants are taught to question the now differentiated components of the situation (e.g., "Is this person really intending to hurt me?" "Is there something else about this situation that is making me angry?"). Finally, in the Resolve step, participants are taught ways to resolve the conflict based on the information they gathered in the Thinking and Questioning steps. These steps can be taught and reinforced through the use of role plays as well as writing the steps on a note card for participants to keep with them

The therapist can facilitate the participant's experience of the activity by using the following questions:
- What are your triggers for anger?
- If I didn't know you, how would I know that you were upset?
- What have you been taught about expressing anger?
- What are some challenges that you have had in adaptively resolving conflict?

Super Dude Therapeutic Story

Treatment Modality: Individual

Goals
- Facilitate discussion about the influence of anger on behavior and thinking.
- Identify strategies for managing anger.

Materials
- Pencil
- Super Dude Therapeutic Story book

Description

The Super Dude Therapeutic Story provides an easily understandable format to discuss the concept of anger with children. The therapist reads the story to the child, encouraging him to think about ways in which he is like Super Dude by highlighting his challenges with anger (e.g., ways in which Mad Man overpowers Super Dude) and his super powers (e.g., ways in which Super Dude is able to defeat Mad Man). The therapist encourages the child to take ownership of the story by having him write down three ways that he can learn to control his anger.

The therapist can facilitate the participant's experience of the activity by using the following questions:
- In what ways are you like Super Dude?
- What challenges do you have controlling anger?
- How can you defeat Mad Man?

Mindful Bingo

Treatment Modality: Group

Goals
- Learn to identify various words associated with mindfulness.
- Facilitate discussion concerning mindfulness practices.
- Improve mindfulness vocabulary and application of mindfulness practices.

Materials
- Bingo Cards (see appendix)
- Bingo Prizes (e.g., candy, small toys)

Description
Participants play the Feelings Bingo game with regular Bingo rules (e.g., five horizontal, vertical, or diagonal signals a winner). To expand the game and move past recognition to description, additional prizes can be awarded for describing how the word is associated with mindfulness and ways that the group member can apply it to the challenges he or she is experiencing.

The therapist can facilitate the participant's experience of the activity by using the following questions:
- What challenges do you face staying in the present moment?
- How can you apply _____ to mindful practices in your life?
- What is the most/least challenging mindfulness concept for you?

Racial/ethnic Identity

"I'm me" collage

Treatment Modality: Individual, Group

Goals
- Facilitate a discussion concerning how the participant defines Blackness for himself.
- Facilitate a discussion of the historical underpinnings of the negative stereotypes associated with being a Black male.
- Encourage self-esteem building utilizing the concept of race.
- Create a tangible reminder of the positive aspects of being a Black male based on the participant's definition.

Materials
- Large poster board
- Scissors
- Pencil
- Markers
- Glue
- Magazines

Description
Black males are chronically exposed to negative impressions of what it means to be a Black male via the media, societal expectations, and racism and discrimination. Several studies have highlighted the importance of defining one's Blackness to mental health and positive racial identity development. This activity will help participants explore who society thinks they are as a Black male vs. what being a Black male means them. The therapist will encourage the participant to make two

collages out of images cut out of magazines that highlight these differing perspectives and discuss.

The therapist can facilitate the participant's experience of the activity by using the following questions:
- What messages have you learned about what it means to be a Black male?
- How have these messages influenced how you interact with other people?
- How have these messages influenced how you think about yourself?
- What does being a Black male mean to you?

ABOUT THE AUTHOR

Steven Kniffley Jr., Psy.D., earned his undergraduate in psychology at the University of Louisville and completed his graduate studies at Spalding University, earning a master's and a doctorate (Psy.D.) in clinical psychology. Steven has also trained as a postdoctoral psychology fellow at Cambridge Health Alliance, a teaching affiliate of Harvard Medical School. As a clinician, researcher, and social activist, Steven is deeply committed to issues related to Black males. Steven's main areas of interest include understanding Black male psychology and the development of multicultural interventions in a clinical setting as well as equipping Black males to succeed in higher education. You can contact Steven at empowerblackmen@gmail.com.

Appendix

		Feelings Bingo		
Relieved	Joy	Mad	Frustrated	Lonely
Guilty	Nervous	Fear	Love	Irritated
Bored	Disappointed	**Emotions** Free Space	Frightened	Angry
Disgusted	Happy	Anxious	Sad	Jealous
Afraid	Cautious	Exhausted	Confident	Surprised

Feelings Bingo

Disgusted	Mad	Relieved	Cautious	Disappointed
Frightened	Nervous	Irritated	Fear	Anxious
Exhausted	Jealous	**Emotions** **Free Space**	Guilty	Joy
Lonely	Bored	Love	Afraid	Surprised
Happy	Confident	Sad	Frustrated	Angry

Feelings Bingo

Irritated	Nervous	Disappointed	Disgusted	Relieved
Anxious	Sad	Confident	Happy	Love
Frightened	Surprised	**Emotions** **Free Space**	Lonely	Frustrated
Afraid	Cautious	Exhausted	Angry	Guilty
Joy	Jealous	Bored	Fear	Mad

Feelings Bingo

Love	Confident	Cautious	Mad	Irritated
Disgusted	Joy	Disappointed	Exhausted	Jealous
Bored	Frightened	**Emotions** Free Space	Fear	Afraid
Surprised	Relieved	Happy	Lonely	Anxious
Nervous	Guilty	Sad	Angry	Frustrated

SUPER DUDE

By:

Once upon a time there was a Super Hero named Super Dude, and he had special super powers… (Draw a picture of what your Super Dude looks like)

Super Dude could fly, and he had super strength! However, Super Dude had an archenemy named MAD MAN…
(Draw a picture of what Mad Man looks like to you)

MAD MAN knew Super Dude's only weakness was when his feelings were out of CONTROL… (Draw a picture of what you look like when you feel out of control)

MAD MAN could make Super Dude so ANGRY that he couldn't use his super powers… (Draw a picture of what you look like when you're angry)

What are three things YOU think Super Dude could do to keep MAD MAN from taking his super powers?
1.)
2.)
3.)

YOU have helped Super Dude defeat MAD MAN! (Draw a picture of Super Dude defeating Mad Man)

My Anxiety Monster

By:

What does your Anxiety Monster look like?

Anxiety Monster's Name:

Draw a picture of how the Anxiety Monster Treats You.

Draw a picture of how the Anxiety Monster makes you feel.

How have you tried to get rid of the Anxiety Monster?

How have they worked?

How would your life be different if the Anxiety Monster wasn't around?

Draw a picture of what this would look like…

Acceptance and Control (remember chocolate cake)

Anxiety is like a roller coaster there will be Highs (which will not last forever), but there will also be Lows.

The Key: Don't ignore the Highs, just know WHEN and WHERE they are coming…

What does your experience tell you about your ability to defeat the Anxiety Monster?

Draw a picture of what this looks like…

Shelldon Takes Time to Stop and Think

(Draw a picture of Shelldon)

My Name Is:

Shelldon Turtle is a terrific turtle. He likes to play with his friends at Swamp Lake School. Draw Shelldon with his friends.

But sometimes things happen that can make Shelldon really mad. What does Shelldon look like when he's mad?

When Shelldon got mad, he used to hit, kick, or yell at his friends. His friends would get mad or upset when he hit, kicked, or yelled at them.

(What do you look like when you're mad?)

Shelldon now knows a new way to "think like a turtle" when he gets mad.

He can STOP and keep his hands, body, and yelling to himself!

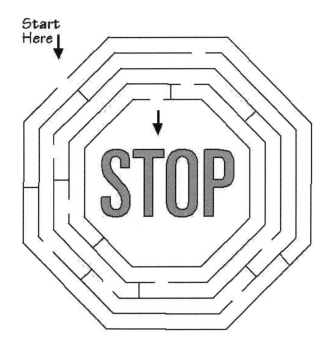

He can TUCK inside his shell and take 3 DEEP BREATHS to calm down. (Draw Shelldon in his shell taking his deep breaths)

Shelldon can then THINK OF A SOLUTION or a way to make it better. What does Shelldon look like when he is thinking?

Shelldon's friends are happy when he plays nicely and keeps his body to himself. Friends also like it when Shelldon uses nice words or has a teacher help him when he is upset.

(Draw you and your friends being happy)

Mindful Bingo

judge	feelings	thoughts	describe	awareness
calm	interpret	commitment	focus	identify
automatic	experience	**Attention** Free Space	breath	notice
control	mindfulness	relax	avoid	facts
present	observe	accept	practice	sensation

Mindful Bingo

present	mindfulness	interpret	sensation	accept
commitment	practice	avoid	facts	calm
describe	judge	**Attention** Free Space	identify	breath
focus	thoughts	feelings	awareness	automatic
experience	observe	notice	relax	control

Mindful Bingo

accept	calm	control	mindfulness	notice
relax	observe	facts	breath	avoid
commitment	practice	**Attention** **Free Space**	interpret	automatic
describe	experience	focus	present	sensation
feelings	judge	awareness	thoughts	identify

Mindful Bingo

awareness	judge	observe	interpret	focus
experience	identify	avoid	mindfulness	thoughts
notice	present	**Attention** Free Space	breath	sensation
control	describe	feelings	automatic	commitment
accept	practice	calm	relax	facts

Made in the USA
Lexington, KY
29 April 2016